Advanced Introduction to Social Capital

Elgar Advanced Introductions are stimulating and thoughtful introductions to major fields in the social sciences, business and law, expertly written by the world's leading scholars. Designed to be accessible yet rigorous, they offer concise and lucid surveys of the substantive and policy issues associated with discrete subject areas.

The aims of the series are two-fold: to pinpoint essential principles of a particular field, and to offer insights that stimulate critical thinking. By distilling the vast and often technical corpus of information on the subject into a concise and meaningful form, the books serve as accessible introductions for undergraduate and graduate students coming to the subject for the first time. Importantly, they also develop well-informed, nuanced critiques of the field that will challenge and extend the understanding of advanced students, scholars and policy-makers.

For a full list of titles in the series please see the back of the book. Recent titles in the series include:

Children's Rights
Gamze Erdem Türkelli and Wouter Vandenhole

Sustainable Careers
Jeffrey H. Greenhaus and Gerard A. Callanan

Business and Human Rights
Peter T. Muchlinski

Spatial Statistics
Daniel A. Griffith and Bin Li

The Sociology of the Self
Shanyang Zhao

Artificial Intelligence in Healthcare
Tom Davenport, John Glaser and Elizabeth Gardner

Central Banks and Monetary Policy
Jakob de Haan and Christiaan Pattipeilohy

Megaprojects
Nathalie Drouin and Rodney Turner

Social Capital
Karen S. Cook

Advanced Introduction to

Social Capital

KAREN S. COOK

Ray Lyman Wilbur Professor of Sociology, Department of Sociology, Stanford University, USA

Elgar Advanced Introductions

Cheltenham, UK • Northampton, MA, USA

Published by
Edward Elgar Publishing Limited
The Lypiatts
15 Lansdown Road
Cheltenham
Glos GL50 2JA
UK

Edward Elgar Publishing, Inc.
William Pratt House
9 Dewey Court
Northampton
Massachusetts 01060
USA

A catalogue record for this book
is available from the British Library

Library of Congress Control Number: 2022941183

ISBN 978 1 78990 267 9 (cased)
ISBN 978 1 78990 269 3 (paperback)
ISBN 978 1 78990 268 6 (eBook)

Printed and bound in Great Britain by TJ Books Limited, Padstow, Cornwall

This book is dedicated to my sons,
Brian and Kevin Cook

Contents

Figures

About the author

KAREN S. COOK is the Ray Lyman Wilbur Professor of Sociology. She is founding Director of the Institute for Research in the Social Sciences (IRiSS) at Stanford and a trustee of the Russell Sage Foundation. Professor Cook has a long-standing interest in social exchange, social networks, social justice, and trust in social relations. She has edited a series of books for the Russell Sage Foundation including *Trust in Society* (2001), *Trust and Distrust in Organizations: Emerging Perspectives* (with R. Kramer, 2004), *eTrust: Forming Relations in the Online World* (with C. Snijders, V. Buskens, and Coye Cheshire, 2009), and *Whom Can You Trust?* (with M. Levi and R. Hardin, 2009). She is co-author of *Cooperation without Trust?* (with R. Hardin and M. Levi, 2005). She has served on the council of the National Academy of Sciences, Engineering and Medicine and as a member of the DBASSE advisory committee. In 1996, she was elected to the American Academy of Arts and Sciences and in 2007 to the National Academy of Sciences. In 2004 she received the ASA Social Psychology Section Cooley Mead Award for Career Contributions to Social Psychology. She was elected a fellow of the American Philosophical Society in 2018.

Preface

This book is in many ways the culmination of a career which began in the early 1970s focused on inequity and fairness, the topic of my dissertation. This fascination with justice and fairness was personal. It led me to subsequent research on power inequality, social networks, and, ultimately, trust. My work on social exchange theory began in graduate school and blossomed at the University of Washington where for a decade I had a very fruitful collaboration with my colleague, Richard Emerson, before his untimely death in 1982. This collaboration also included a life-long friendship with Toshio Yamagishi, a scholar's scholar and highly accomplished academic who spent most of his career at Hokkaido University in Sapporo. Mary Rogers Gillmore, a noted researcher who applied her deep knowledge of sociology to social work in important ways, was also one of our key team members as we built one of the first computerized labs for the study of social interaction and social networks in the nation. Over a long career I have had many other fruitful collaborations, often with current and former students, too numerous at this point to list here.

It is not surprising, given the nature of my publications over the years, that I chose to accept this invitation to write about social capital, encompassing the study of networks, norms, and trust. I thank the Russell Sage Foundation, particularly former president Eric Wanner, for supporting the working group on trust and the subsequent workshops and book series on trust which lasted over a decade or so. It is this collaboration that led me to focus my research on the role of trust in society for over two decades. As I hope this book makes clear, trust is an important element in any working society. It fosters cooperation, collective action, and social cohesion, much needed in a world divided by crises fueled by pandemics, political conflicts, and environmental challenges. While Robert Putnam put the analysis of social capital (and its elements) on the policy agenda more than two decades ago, I hope this volume continues to inspire research that will help meet the challenges we face in the coming decades as a nation and as a member of the international community.

Karen S. Cook
Stanford, California

Acknowledgments

This book began as a sabbatical project just before the global pandemic shut down the world in March of 2020. I am grateful to have had the time to work on this book, while spending most of it at home, somewhat isolated from the usual joys of academic life including travel, conferences, and teaching. I want to thank Stanford University for the resources it provides faculty engaged in research and writing, particularly for the time it offers us periodically for deeper engagement with our work. I also received support from the Institute for Research in the Social Sciences (IRiSS) at Stanford, while I was serving as its faculty director during the final stages of writing this book. The Institute is located in the hills above Stanford and is an ideal place for contemplation. It also has a remarkable staff, some of whom helped when computer issues slowed progress toward completion. I want to thank Chris Thomsen, the Executive Director of IRiSS, for his many years of support and leadership. I also want to thank the various editors at Edward Elgar who managed to keep this book on their radar screen through several staffing changes. Finally, I thank my extended family for making work on this book not only possible but fun, especially Kendall and Kaia, whose distractions were always welcome.

1 Social capital: an introduction

> Social capital is "features of social organization, such as *trust, norms and networks*, that can improve efficiency of society by facilitating coordinated actions."
> (Putnam, Leonardi, and Nanetti 1993: 167)

Social capital has been defined in various ways in the social sciences, including in the quote above from the work of Robert Putnam, a political scientist who spent most of his career at Harvard. But the term "social capital" currently has no singular meaning that is broadly accepted. The earliest uses of the concept can be found in the works of social scientists such as Jane Jacobs (1961), Glenn Loury (1977), Pierre Bourdieu (1986), and James S. Coleman (1988). Loury (1977), for example, argues importantly that success for individuals is not simply based on their human capital or inherent abilities. These chances for success are distributed unevenly in society and certainly have social origins. The social situations in which individuals are embedded matter in terms of the development of their human capital. Access to opportunity is socially structured. Networks that link people to resources, opportunities, and norms of cooperation at the local level as well as the existence of general social trust make a difference not only for individuals, but also for organizations, communities, and society at large. Research on social capital focuses on a wide range of related topics exploring the positive and negative effects of these fundamentally social factors – networks, norms, and trust.

Beyond these modern origins of the concept, it was Robert Putnam (1995a, 1995b) who popularized the concept by proclaiming alarm at the decline of *social capital* in America that could threaten its democratic institutions at the close of the twentieth century. Little did he know how prophetic his concerns would become. Sources of evidence for this bold claim included, but were not limited to, a decrease in membership in civic associations such as the parent–teacher association (PTA) and other volunteer organizations, as well as an increase in social isolation and "bowling alone" (Putnam 1995b, 2000), in addition to lower rates of voting as well as disengagement from the political process in general, all potentially leading to the demise of civil society with somewhat dire consequences.

In the late 1990s, such claims got the attention not only of social scientists but also those in government in the United States as well as in other democratic countries, particularly in Europe. Putnam (2000: 349) declared that "The performance of our democratic institutions depends in measurable ways upon social capital." Besides declining social capital, other perceived threats to the health of democratic institutions, and to social cohesion more broadly, subsequently articulated by Putnam (2007), included increasing immigration and the migration of workers and refugees across porous borders around the globe. This international trend continues due both to climate change and its local effects as well as to intergroup conflict and warfare. In the United States, hopeful and often desperate migrants now camp at many of its southern borders waiting for asylum.

The claim in Putnam's work is that the resulting increase in ethnic heterogeneity in cities and neighborhoods in various regions of the United States would lead to a breakdown in social cohesion and the kind of general social trust that had existed in more homogeneous communities (Putnam 2007; Dinesen, Schaeffer, and Sonderskov 2020; but see also Portes and Vickstrom 2011). According to Putnam, individuals under these circumstances "hunker down," failing to take a risk on those who are "different" from themselves, reducing social ties within the community, and weakening social bonds. General social trust suffers. I address this specific claim and the related evidence for it in subsequent chapters.

To some extent, in 2022, some of these claims about civic participation seem somewhat "quaint." In the aftermath of a global pandemic, rampant nationalism, ever-expanding critical environmental crises, and increasing threats to democracies all over the world, concerns over too much bowling alone and not enough engagement in the PTA or similar civic associations pale. But that conclusion would be shortsighted. Forms of social capital can be seen to have either exacerbated the situation or helped in creating solutions to some of these significant challenges to society. This will become evident as we begin to clarify how to think about social capital and its role in society, as well as how to conceptualize it and produce the kinds of evidence relevant to the many claims made about its effects, both positive and negative.

1.1   Social capital: networks, norms, and trust

In Putnam's original conception (1993: 167) provided in his co-authored book with Leonardi and Nanettii on making democracy work, *social capital* is referred to as "features of social organization, such as *trust, norms and networks*, that can improve the efficiency of society by facilitating coordinated actions." It is this version of the definition that has gained criticism (see also Cook 2005) in part because it makes it clear that it is best considered an "umbrella" term that includes related concepts that are very broad and incorporate large swaths of social science. What Putnam did in a big way, however, was to raise alarm about the future of democracy and civil society. Importantly, he brought social science into the mainstream consciousness of the public as well as politicians and governmental leaders, not to mention to those engaged with non-profits and other organizations dealing with major societal concerns. In many ways he anticipated the malaise that some democracies around the globe, but especially America, are currently facing.

In his work, Putnam raises significant and broad-reaching concerns that go to the heart of democratic institutions and their viability given ongoing critical challenges relating to polarization, voting rights, diversity, nationalism, international conflicts, climate change, and now, more than ever, public health. His voice is steady and merits attention. In more recent work, he comments on how our kids are faring in a society increasingly characterized by deepening inequality and the intergenerational transmission of poverty. He has also written a manifesto in his book, *The Upswing*, on how we can return to a more "we-centered" society (Putnam 2020). His many contributions to the social sciences and humanities have earned him many significant prizes and well-deserved honors including the National Humanities Medal given to him by then president Barack Obama. He continues to identify sweeping social and political trends important to the future of democracies and to offer panaceas for despair and division (Putnam 2020).

The work on social capital, broadly defined, over the past three decades has increased at a rapid pace following Putnam's lead. One analysis shows that the number of publications that include social capital as a focus has been rising steeply since the term was popularized in the 1990s. Even simply listing the main references to the separate literatures on "networks, norms, and trust" would fill the pages of a book. And by now there are thousands of studies in many countries reporting on social capital in various parts of the world. Such a broad conception of social capital as that proposed by Putnam makes it difficult to find clarity of meaning in the term or in its empirical referents (Paxton 1999; Portes 2000; Fischer 2005). In fact, a large number of contributors to the literature on social capital have made this point and they have dealt with these issues by creating their own definitions and measures, making it hard to compare results. While there is no agreement yet on a precise definition, what most treatments of social capital have in common is a focus on *social connections* in groups or networks and the various resources that can be obtained through such connections. It is these useful links to others that we value and work to create as well as maintain.

For Bourdieu (1986: 248) social capital is "the aggregate of the actual or potential resources which are linked to possession of a *durable network* of more or less institutionalized relationships of mutual acquaintance and recognition or ... to membership in a group that provides each of its members with the backing of the collectivity-owned capital ..." and the credentials that ensure credit. His primary focus was on the stability of stratification systems in society and how "dominant class reproduction" is legitimized. An important element in his work is the focus on differential access to the *cultural capital* linked to social class that facilitates and sustains class reproduction. It also limits opportunity. Cultural capital has a major effect on educational and thus occupational outcomes, for example. It is clearly unequally distributed.

Coleman (1988) treats social capital as inherent in social structures and as a source of resources (including information, support, shared norms, and social control) that are available through membership, association, or other forms of *social connection*. He emphasized the value to members of closed networks or groups with boundaries, connections that facilitate certain actions of those involved, particularly collective actions of mutual benefit, in some ways harkening back to the past. According to Marsden (2005: 15), "For Coleman (1988: S98), social capital refers to features of social structure that facilitate action. Among these are systems of *trust* and obligations, *networks* disseminating information, *norms* accompanied by sanctioning systems, centralized authority structures arising through transfers of control." Marsden (2005: 15) goes on to clarify that Coleman[1] also must have regarded the concept of social capital as "more of a covering term for 'useful social organization' than as an identifiable 'variable,' given its reference to such a variety of forms of social capital," similar in this respect to Putnam's subsequent treatment of the term.

Other theorists have provided variants of these earlier definitions of social capital. Some variants retain breadth; others are simplified, often to make the concept operational in research. In his important book on social trust in which he makes cross-national comparisons, Fukuyama (1995: 26) states that "Social capital is a capability that arises from the prevalence of *trust* in a society or in certain parts of it." He argues for its significance in facilitating collective action and the extension of social interaction beyond families and close circles of acquaintances laying the foundation for economic growth. So, for Fukuyama, general social trust is a good indicator of the existence of social capital in society. He talks about networks and norms in his discussion of general social trust and its role in economic development, but his focus is on trust as social capital and its effects mainly in the realm of economics. Some economists have followed suit. Restricting the definition to one key aspect is a strategy that many subsequent researchers have adopted in order to find appropriate measures and to employ the concept directly in research efforts.

A somewhat more common approach in some fields than the one taken by Fukuyama (1995) is the effort to limit the focus to *networks*, making them the key aspect of social capital to be investigated. Portes (1998: 6) concludes that, despite differences, "the consensus is growing that social capital stands for the ability of actors to secure benefits by virtue of membership in social networks or other social structures." Sandefur and Laumann (1998) also argue for such a focus, directing attention to the basic role of social relationships and the structures they form. According to Sandefur and Laumann (1998: 484), a person's "stock of social capital consists of the collection and pattern of relationships in which she is involved and to which she has access, and further to the location and patterning of her associations in larger social space." These relationships are the source of the resources including information, influence and control, and social solidarity, which Sandefur and Laumann identify as the "benefits" of social capital. They note, however, that the effects of access to such social capital are not always positive. Negative outcomes may also exist – a possibility that researchers refer to as the "dark side" of social capital (Portes 1998; Putnam 2000; Cook 2005). Portes (1998: 8) defines social capital similarly, focusing on social structures, including networks, that provide benefits. He also makes clear the extent to which social capital can be used for nefarious purposes as well as the more positive provision of social goods (individual or collective). Nothing assures us that it will be put to good uses in society.

Nan Lin and his collaborators took a related tack addressing the location and patterning of social relationships yielded by stratification in a society that facilitates or limits access to those in specific social positions and the resources they control. Lin (2001: 3) argues that theory and research on the topic of social capital needs to be "based on the fundamental understanding that social capital is captured from *embedded resources in social networks.*" This clarity makes it easier both to understand what it is and to measure it. As further noted by Lin (2001: 6), "The premise behind the notion of social capital is rather simple … *investment in social relations with expected returns.*" It is this notion of social capital that has been picked up ardently in the popular media and is often referred to as "networking" in everyday parlance.

What matters most in networks are the positions one occupies, the nature of the connections to others in the network, and the resources (including information and influence) inherent in and accessible from one's location. Social capital often references the fact that networks of social relationships serve as resources for both individuals and for society in terms of facilitating collective action. Thus, network conceptions of social capital are common in the general literature on social capital, its origins, and effects (Stolle 2007). They are also the most straightforward (see also Foley and Edwards 1999). As Mouw (2006: 79) argues: "The key concept here is that social capital is not an individual characteristic or a personality trait but a resource that resides in the networks and groups to which people belong." Even Putnam (2000: 19) concurs when he states clearly that "the *core idea* of social capital theory is that social networks have value." We focus attention on this core idea.

This book is divided into three main sections. Each examines one of the three pillars that Putnam (1995b) identified as components of social capital – *networks, norms,* and *trust.* I do this to give a more complete introduction to the factors that have been defined as significant in the broad literature on social capital. No single book has done or will do justice to the many ways in which this construct has been applied in the social sciences. A few handbooks and reviews exist that provide a sense of the breadth of inquiry into the content, causes, and consequences of social capital for individuals and for society (e.g., Halpern 2005; Castiglione, van Deth, and Woller 2008; Svendsen and Svendsen 2009; Jones 2019), even though it is not possible to summarize it all in any single volume. All I can do in this book is provide an introduction to the topic and its significance for social science as well as society at large.

1.2   Declining social capital?

Before moving to a discussion of networks, the central component of social capital in my view, I review some of the main arguments that have emerged about social capital including the earlier work of Putnam (1995a, 1995b, 2000, 2002; see also Putnam, Leonardi, and Nanetti 1993) that spawned the surge in research and writing on this topic across the social sciences as well as in popular media outlets. We begin with comments on the claim that social capital in the United States is in decline and that such a decline is problematic for the future of democracy, an argument Robert Putnam made at the dawn of the twenty-first century. We then review just a few of the wide-ranging criticisms of this work before moving on to talk about networks and social relationships as sources of social capital in Chapter 2. In this chapter we will talk about the consequences of having or not having access to the resources derived from networks, and the determinants of this inequality in access to the core component of social capital.

For Putnam (1994, 1995a) the main argument is that strong traditions of civic engagement are the bedrock of healthy democracies. This thesis derives from his work on Italy (Putnam, Leonardi, and Nanetti 1993). As Stolle (2007: 660) notes: "The most prominent research finding here results, of course, from Putnam's earlier work on Italy, which shows that networks of civic engagement and resulting generalized trust and norms of reciprocity foster the better performance of regional democratic governments." In his book on the determinants of good governance, Putnam and his co-authors compare northern and southern Italy, attempting to unearth factors that are linked to better government and higher levels of economic growth. Later, he applies these lessons learned to an analysis of government institutions in the United States, arguing that the decline in civic engagement is detrimental to community life, to political and social institutions, and a worrisome source of democratic instability.

In 2021, it can be said that democratic institutions have certainly been under attack in various parts of the world including, perhaps most notably, the United States. But it is not at all clear that such developments on the world stage can be attributed primarily to a decline in social capital or civic engagement as originally put forth by Putnam. Other political and social forces have emerged in recent decades. The rise of inequality, polarization, nationalism, climate migration, immigration, and international conflict are among such forces.

Let us review just a few of Putnam's primary claims more closely and then discuss some of the research that refutes them, setting aside for the moment more theoretical and methodological issues with such claims and the related literature on social capital. The real focus of Putnam's work, growing out of his analysis of regional government in Italy, is that civic engagement builds networks of association that foster solidarity and reinforce norms of reciprocity and demonstrations of trustworthiness which in turn support collaboration and commitment to the public good. "When economic and political dealing is embedded in dense networks of social interaction, incentives for opportunism and malfeasance are reduced" (Putnam 1994: 37).

Civic engagement in his research includes a broad range of activities such as participation in volunteer organizations, religious institutions, and community associations; voting and other political activities; even communal sports activities,[2] all of which create social ties and serve as conduits of information, influence, and connection. In subsequent cross-national research, Paxton (2002) finds that the specific characteristics of such associations matter in terms of their effects on democratic institutions. Those voluntary associations that offer connections among people more directly, such as bird-watching organizations, produce positive effects whereas those that are more isolated do not and, in fact, may have negative effects. These effects depend on what the associations do.

Putnam focuses on the positive outcomes of high levels of social capital, though he does acknowledge that there is a dark side as well (Putnam 2000). In his sweeping review of a wide range of data in which he identifies trends in the decline of social capital during the last few decades of the twentieth century, he discusses several ways in which "social capital works its magic" (Putnam 2000: 288–9). These include the resolution of collective action problems by way of social norms and the "networks that enforce them," as well as the trust that builds in communities in which repeated interactions facilitate norm enforcement and the commitment to reciprocity.

The networks not only support norms of collective behavior for the common good – they also serve as conduits for information that is useful, often in the achievement of personal goals (such as obtaining a new job or a daycare referral: see Small 2009). Granovetter's (1974) earlier work on referral networks for jobs had already established the role of connections for positive employment outcomes. In fact, his research demonstrated that even "weak," more distant, and less intense ties serve this purpose, typically more effectively than "strong" network ties, linking close friends and family, since the latter may involve more redundant information and are less far-reaching. This work fostered a research enterprise on the role of network ties in employment and other domains that continues to this day (cf., Granovetter 1983).

In the various domains mentioned above, Putnam argues there is evidence of a decline in participation replaced to some extent by less social activities such as gaming and other Internet activities or watching TV, frequently alone (activities that increased exponentially during the global pandemic several decades later). Political participation and other civic activities declined over the last two decades of the twentieth century, at the time Putnam was writing his main opus on social capital. From data charts, he concludes (2000: 41): "The frequency of virtually every form of community involvement measured in the Roper polls declined significantly, from the most common – petition signing – to the least common – running for office" from the 1960s to the end of the twentieth century. Putnam (2000: 412) reaches the conclusion that "Nowhere is the need to restore connectedness, trust and civic engagement clearer than in the now often empty public forums of our democracy." And this statement preceded the political turmoil that eventually ended in 2021 in riots in the seat of U.S. government, driven by deep political animosity and unhealthy partisanship.

Even religious participation had decreased during the last third of the twentieth century, as indicated both by church attendance and membership, though it decreased more in certain regions of the United States (i.e., the West) than in others. Despite growing interest in fundamentalistic sects over time, general participation in religious activities declined. Putnam makes the argument that this is, in part, generational. The large cohorts of baby boomers were much less likely to attend church or join one than many in their parents' generation, those who lived through World War II and had to "step-up" to defend their country against invasion. That generation was later venerated by Tom Brokaw (2001) and others as the "Greatest Generation" due to their collective commitment to action during the war and afterward to rebuild a great society.

Accompanying reported declines in civic, political, and religious participation, Putnam argues that workplace connections frayed, fewer informal social connections were made as a result of dinners or outings with neighbors and friends, and rates of volunteering and philanthropic acts dropped. All of these factors contributed to the overall disengagement from civic actions and the lower levels of the trust and general reciprocity that come with informal connections and ties to one another. A consequence (or corollary) is that formal institutions and legal remedies end up filling in where once informal networks and trust were central to accomplishing collective tasks, often increasing transaction costs and undermining social cohesion.

Against these notable trends, Putnam (2000: 180) summarized a few exceptions, including an increase in volunteering among young people, an increase in some forms of social and organizational connection through the Internet, the growth of self-help and other types of support groups, as well as greater engagement in religious groups primarily by the more evangelical conservatives. What followed Putnam's early work was a tsunami of studies aimed at verifying or refuting his claims, as well as efforts to evaluate the underlying theoretical arguments and to clarify policy implications.

1.3   Conceptual and measurement issues

As we noted in the introduction, the main criticism of the concept social capital as Putnam defined it is that it is too broad and includes concepts best defined and measured separately – networks, norms, and trust. Putting them all under the umbrella "social capital" brings attention to the topic but does not form a strong basis for clear conceptualizations and analysis. In fact, it is often hard to assess what we know and do not know about social capital in the existing literature despite many attempts at assessment specifically because the concept is murky, and investigators tend to use the data at hand to provide measures, typically derived from surveys of individuals (cf., Portes 2000; Durlauf 2002; Sobel 2002; Durlauf and Fafchamps 2005) often from General Social Surveys (GSS) in various countries or the World Values Surveys (WVS).

Other researchers have tried to develop their own measures of social capital, typically separating individual and collective sources (cf., Lochner, Kawachi, and Kennedy 1999; Narayan and Cassidy 2001; Grootaert, Narayan, Jones, and Woolcock 2004). And given the multi-dimensional nature of the concept, social capital, some have argued that a mixed-methods approach to studying it would be especially useful, including both quantitative measures as well as qualitative approaches to understanding the underlying nature of the concepts and processes involved (see Jones and Woolcock 2009). The economist Solow (1995: 36) writes early on that "If 'social capital' is to be more than a buzzword, something more than mere relevance or even importance is required. ... The stock of social capital should somehow be measurable, even if inexactly".

One compelling critique of Putnam's argument about the decline of social capital demonstrates several ways in which definitions and measures matter. Paxton (1999) attempts to answer the simple question: "Is social capital declining in the United States?" Putnam (2000) presents a large amount of descriptive data up through the late 1990s indicating declines in aspects of social capital such as memberships in unions and profes-sional associations, church membership and attendance, club meeting attendance, service on committees and the administration of local school or town organizations, as well as voting and participation in political organizations and campaigns, among other indicators. These trends, he argues, may also be exacerbated by increasing social isolation in living arrangements as more people live alone. Other factors include increases in parallel rather than interactive forms of engagement with the growth of the Internet over time and the rapid increase in screen time (i.e., TV, computers, and cell phones, etc.), a trend that increased almost exponentially as cell phones subsequently became readily available worldwide and several decades later a global pandemic forced people to work from home.

In the book *Bowling Alone*, Putnam (2000) includes information on his comprehensive Social Capital Index that has been used in many studies of the effects of waning social capital. This index includes measures of various components including indicators of involvement with organizational life at the community level (i.e., clubs and local groups), engagement in public affairs (e.g., elections), extent of various types of community volunteerism, as well as questions about informal sociability and standard measures of social trust. These factors are fairly highly correlated, enough such that Putnam was able to include them jointly in his index of overall level of social capital which varies significantly, for example, across the states in the U.S.A. In subsequent work many researchers, using different measures and methods, have tried to separate out the distinct as well as the joint effects of these factors.

As an early critic of Putnam's thesis of declining social capital, Paxton (1999) identified several problems with both the measures of social capital and the prior analyses of the data on trends (see also Stolle and Hooghe 2005). In fact, in her study she finds no decline in engagement with social associations or with trust in institutions, though she does find a decline in trust in individuals (see also Clark 2015). In this work, trust is included as a form of social capital as part of Putnam's original concept. Many social and political theorists have argued at various points in history that there is a growing lack of community that threatens democratic institutions, so the general alarm sounded by Putnam was not new in social science. But this is precisely the fear that Putnam reinvigorated at the end of the twentieth century. What Paxton does is to critique not only the conceptualization of social capital, but also the factors used as indicators of social capital and the underlying causal arguments that had been proposed.

1.4   A closer look

To clarify the focus of her analysis, Paxton treats trust and engagement with associations and related community ties as separate components in her model. Using a sophisticated measurement model for both components she finds no real decline in her measures of association (with friends, neighbors, and groups) using data from the mid-1970s to the late 1990s (from the GSS in each year). With respect to trust, she separates trust in individuals from trust in institutions (e.g., education, government, religious organizations) and finds different trends.[3] Over the time frame she examines, there is first an increase in trust in institutions and then a moderate decrease but, overall, very little change in institutional confidence (a fact that has changed in more recent decades). The main trend is a decline in trust in other individuals which she later argues may be reflected in changes in society at that time, such as the increase in gated communities in various regions of the United States. Putnam and others have argued that this effect may be associated primarily with generational change. That is, the older, more trusting cohorts of citizens are being replaced over time with less trusting individuals, growing up under different conditions (but see Clark 2015).

When combining the trust and association membership components together to model the overall decline in social capital including both components, Paxton finds a decrease during the time frame she analyzes although it is primarily driven by the consistent decline in trust in individuals over time. Her findings indicate that when social capital is considered as a complex mix of components it is hard to pin down exactly which factors are causing changes over time, especially if there are not clear and separate indicators of the various aspects of social capital. To ignore this problem is to obfuscate what is meant in the end by changes in aggregate levels of "social capital." Is it a change in trust in institutions, trust in individuals, spending time with neighbors or friends, joining associations (social or political), or some other indicator of civic engagement? And, Paxton does not focus on the network aspect of social capital, in part because the data she aggregates are individual-level responses to the GSS over a specific time frame, not network-level data that is not routinely collected in the GSS. Those who do focus on networks (see Chapter 2) also suggest that, in addition to clarity of meaning and measurement, the choice of data analysis techniques is critical to being able to assess the actual effects of social capital of various types on outcomes that matter (see Mouw 2006 for details on causality inferences).

Several reasons have been proposed in the research on social capital for why membership in voluntary associations may not promote civic responsibility or positive citizenship behaviors. For example, in addressing this argument, Theiss-Morse and Hibbing (2005) note that not all groups promote democratic values. As evident in various countries in Europe, for instance, as well as in the United States, certain associations espouse anti-democratic and authoritarian values instead. For this reason, civic participation does not always lead to and may turn people away from political participation. It may partially account for low rates of voting in democratic countries and disengagement from politics more generally.

A related factor is the tendency for people to join groups that are homogeneous, not heterogeneous, thus reducing their exposure to diverse viewpoints and fostering what have come to be called "echo chambers" in which individuals begin to endorse evermore similar views without exposure to differing perspectives. These echo chambers are in part responsible for increasing polarization in many countries, including the United States. Thiess-Morse and Hibbing (2005: 227) argue that it is very important for "good citizens to learn that democracy is messy, inefficient, and conflict-ridden." This is harder to do in the absence of relevant information (or in the presence of misinformation) and the lack of acknowledgment of legitimate differences in interests and policy preferences requiring compromise. And compromise is increasingly hard to come by in the world of politics in many countries.

In a review of the findings related to the role of involvement with voluntary associations in fostering civic engagement and generating social trust, Newton (2007: 357) sums it up as follows: "voluntary associations do not seem to matter," while acknowledging the fact that they may count in other ways. He goes on to clarify that "most individual and aggregate studies find little support for the idea that membership of, or activity in, voluntary associations generate social trust" (one of the three components of social capital in Putnam's definition).

Research efforts to examine social capital trends, their causes, and consequences are ubiquitous and the results vary depending on which component of social capital is the focus of analysis and the nature of the data brought to bear on the debates surrounding this topic. For example, in the multidisciplinary volume the *Handbook of Social Capital*, edited by Svendsen and Svendsen (2009), social capital is operationalized primarily as trust, which is more common in economics and political science. Political theorist Fukuyama (1995), as we have noted, considers generalized trust in society as the main form of social capital that helps to explain cross-cultural differences in economic growth. Other political scientists focus on assessing what role social capital plays in making democracies work.

Economists often take the same approach in attempting to link social capital with variation in economic development across the globe. Bjornskov (2009: 337), an economist, notes that "... features under the umbrella of social capital are associated with a number of beneficial outcomes such as educational volume, (lack of) corruption, institutional quality and subjective well-being. Perhaps, most importantly, one of these outcomes is the speed with which countries develop economically." Bjornskov goes on to summarize some of the findings on Putnam's core hypothesis about the effects of the decline in social capital, mainly focused on lower levels of civic engagement or connections to associations of differing types (i.e., social versus political). A variety of studies (e.g., Knack 2003) find little support for the positive effects of social capital in terms of membership in associations and related forms of civic engagement (see also Paxton 1999; Clark 2015). As Bjornskov (2009: 339) puts it in discussing Knack's findings: "... the beneficial 'Putnamesque' effects of social capital are probably outweighed by the negative effects of associations working as predatory special interests, as first stressed by Olson (1965)."

In cross-cultural studies, Knack (2003) and others find different and more positive effects of trust, in particular on economic outcomes including economic growth, as we discuss in subsequent chapters on networks and trust. The focus on economic development and growth comes out of Putnam's original study of different economic trajectories of northern and southern Italy. Bjornskov (2009: 347) notes that his own research on cross-country differences in rates of economic growth supports others' findings about the connection between social trust and growth and the lack of connection between associational activity and growth. It also provides support for the large number of empirical studies that conclude that Putnam's three social capital elements are actually separate phenomena.

The economists move on to explain specifically why social trust is associated with economic development, building to some extent on Fukuyama's (1995) thesis. In Bjornskov's (2009) review, he concludes that the specific transmission mechanisms linking social trust and growth include the quality of the existing formal institutions, legal systems, and public bureaucracies as well as increases in education at the population level. Social trust is higher with stronger legal remedies for failed trust and the existence of legitimate institutions that serve as a kind of insurance backing economic transactions and investments. Increases in levels of education raise the capacity of individuals to engage in such transactions and make relevant investments that benefit the society and economic development more directly. Knack and Keefer (1997) find a positive association between social trust and the productivity of workers, another direct effect on economic growth. We delve into this literature more fully in Chapter 4.

1.5   Concluding remarks

Interestingly, some of the research on social capital views trends in the United States as distinct from trends in other countries, an assessment that has been described as "American exceptionalism." In the remaining chapters, we discuss this viewpoint and present some comparative evidence of the effects of social capital (and its forms) in various cultural contexts. Variations in social trust across countries are quite large and are associated with factors such as government performance, political stability, level of inequality in the society, corruption, and economic growth, among others (e.g., Stolle and Hooghe 2005). As an example, Krishna (2002), in a study of more than 60 villages in northern India, finds that social capital (i.e., networks and associations with strong leaders) supports collective actions that facilitate economic development and strengthen democratic institutions. Many other studies focus on the various ways in which elements of social capital matter in different parts of the globe.

Halpern (2005) argues that part of what differentiates countries in terms of social capital reserves (mainly networks and trust) is the shift in underlying values to more individualistic and less collectivistic orientations and a kind of disengagement from those outside one's own social circle. While he views this trend as part of a longer-term historical trajectory that has transformed social relationships more generally "from the 'thick trust' of the traditional community to the 'thin' but powerful trust of the modern society" (Halpern 2005: 243), he also reports on cross-national differences in these overall trends. Societies like the U.S.A., Australia and the U.K. seem to lead the trend, whereas countries like Sweden, the Netherlands and Japan, he argues, buck the trend, demonstrating an increase in trust and activities such as volunteering and informal socializing.

According to Halpern, we do not fully know the causes of these differences, but they are identified by him as including factors at various levels of analysis from the micro, individual level, to the meso and more macro levels in society. These factors focus on personality, class, family, work, and education at the individual level, as well as mobility, community-level forces and ethnic/racial heterogeneity at the meso level, and culture, economic inequality, and welfare state policies at the macro level (among others). We explore some of these factors in the chapters that follow.

In the concluding chapter of *Bowling Alone*, Putnam suggests that naming the problem is the first step toward solution. For him the problem is the disappearance of social capital in the form of engagement with civic associations and the connections they foster that create goodwill, public-mindedness, and a commitment to the public good rather than the relentless pursuit of private goods. Building on what worked during the Progressive Era, he argues that we need to create new forms of social organization that enable and encourage civic engagement, as well as "fortify our resolve as individuals to reconnect" to "overcome the familiar paradox of collective action" (Putnam 2000: 403). The challenge he puts forth is the restoration of "American community for the twenty-first century through both collective and individual initiative." Given the range of challenges facing the world as we move into the second decade of this century, it is not at all clear that we have created the kinds of community that form the basis for a revival of connectedness and caring. It is particularly difficult in the face of global pandemics and the ravages of climate change. To move forward we will need to be clear about the nature of the problems we face and the ways in which the various dimensions of social capital work to facilitate progress.

In order to contribute to understanding the way forward, in this book I focus separately on the three components of what Putnam referred to as social capital: *networks*, *norms*, and *trust*. In this way I hope it becomes clearer what it is that we now know about the significance of these key dimensions of society for the challenges we face, as well as to identify what we have yet to learn. This approach also helps to clarify what we mean when we talk about social capital in each chapter.

In line with an interesting assessment of the social capital literature offered by Woolcock (2010), when the citations of that term in the social science literature reached close to 20,000 over a decade or so, he argues that we should not hold out for a singular definition of the concept. In his words, "… its coherence and usefulness rest not on a clear consensus regarding its definition and measurement, but on its capacity to draw attention to salient features of the social and political world … that play a role in the valued aspects of everyday life (such as education, health and crime prevention" (Woolcock 2010: 470). I agree. But I also agree with him that it thus remains incumbent on investigators to be clear about what they mean when they use the term and to specify how they are measuring it. Let's proceed to talk about the key dimensions of social capital.

Notes

1. "Social capital is defined by its function, it is not a single entity, but a variety of different entities having characteristics in common: they all consist of some aspect of a social structure, and they facilitate certain actions of individuals who are within the structure" (Coleman 1990: 302).
2. Uslaner (2009) even argues that engagement with sports activities is a potential way to rebuild cohesion. I would argue, however, that it might also fuel intergroup rivalries and stoke group conflict, rather than creating grounds for solidarity.
3. Other researchers have also worked on analyzing the different trends over time in the various components of social capital. Schwadel and Stout (2012), for instance, find different trends in these components over 40 years in the United States based on exploring age, period, and cohort effects more thoroughly.

References

Bjornskov, Christian (2009). "Economic Growth." Pp. 337–53 in Gert Tinggaard Svendsen and Gunnar Lind Haase Svendsen (eds.), *Handbook of Social Capital*. Cheltenham, UK and Northampton, MA, USA: Edward Elgar Publishing.

Bourdieu, Pierre (1986). "The Forms of Social Capital." Pp. 241–58 in J. Richardson (ed.) *Handbook of Theory and Research in the Sociology of Education*. New York: Greenwood Press.

Brokaw, Tom (2001). *The Greatest Generation*. New York: Random House.

Castiglione, Dario, Jan W. van Deth, and Guglielmo Woller (2008). *The Handbook of Social Capital*. New York: Oxford University Press.

Clark, April K. (2015). "Rethinking the Decline in Social Capital." *American Politics Research* 43(4): 569–601.

Coleman, James S. (1988). "Social Capital in the Creation of Human Capital." *American Journal of Sociology* 94: S95–S120.

Coleman, James S. (1990). *Foundations of Social Theory*. Cambridge, MA: Harvard University Press.

Cook, Karen S. (2005). "Networks, Norms and Trust: The Social Psychology of Social Capital." *Social Psychology Quarterly* 68(1): 4–14.

Dinesen, Peter Thisted, Merlin Schaeffer, and Kim Mannemar Sonderskov (2020). "Ethnic Diversity and Social Trust: A Narrative and Meta-Analytical Review." *Annual Review of Political Science* 23: 441–65.

Durlauf, Steven N. (2002). "On the Empirics of Social Capital." *The Economic Journal* 112(483): 459–79.

Durlauf, Steven N. and Marcel Fafchamps (2005). "Social Capital." Pp. 1639–99 in Philippe Aghion and Steven N. Durlauf (eds.), *Handbook of Economic Growth*. Amsterdam: Elsevier.

Fischer, Claude S. (2005). "Bowling Alone: What's the Score?" *Social Networks* 27: 155–67.

Foley, Michael W. and Bob Edwards (1999). "Is it Time to Disinvest in Social Capital?" *Journal of Public Policy* 19(2): 141–73.

Fukuyama, Frances (1995). *Trust: The Social Virtues and the Creation of Prosperity*. New York: Penguin.

Granovetter, Mark (1974). *Getting a Job: A Study of Contacts and Careers*. Cambridge, MA: Harvard University Press.

Granovetter, Mark (1983). "The Strength of Weak Ties: A Network Theory Revisited." *Sociological Theory* 1: 201–33.

Grootaert, C., D. Narayan, V.N. Jones, and M. Woolcock (2004). "Measuring Social Capital: An Integrated Questionnaire." *World Bank Working Paper No. 18*. Washington, DC: World Bank.

Halpern, David (2005). *Social Capital*. Cambridge: Polity Press.

Jacobs, Jane (1961). *The Death and Life of Great American Cities*. New York: Random House.

Jones, Brian J. (2019). *Social Capital in American Life*. Cham: Palgrave Pivot (Springer).

Jones, Veronica Nyhan and Michael Woolcock (2009). "Mixed Methods Assessment." Pp. 379–401 in Gert T. Svendsen and Gunnar Lind Haase

Svendsen (eds.), *The Handbook of Social Capital: The Troika of Sociology, Political Science and Economics*. Cheltenham, UK and Northampton, MA, USA: Edward Elgar Publishing.

Knack, Stephen (2003). "Groups, Growth and Trust: Cross-country Evidence on the Olson and Putnam Hypothesis." *Public Choice* 117: 341–55.

Knack, Stephen and Philip Keefer (1997). "Does Social Capital Have an Economic Pay-off? A Cross-country Investigation." *Quarterly Journal of Economics* 112: 1251–88.

Krishna, Anirudh (2002). *Active Social Capital: Tracing the Roots of Development and Democracy*. New York: Columbia University Press.

Lin, Nan (2001). "Building a Network Theory of Social Capital." Pp. 3–29 in N. Lin, K. Cook, and R.S. Burt (eds.), *Social Capital: Theory and Research*. New York: Aldine de Gruyter.

Lochner, Kimberly, Ichiro Kawachi, and Bruce P. Kennedy (1999). "Social Capital: A Guide to its Measurement." *Health and Place* 5(4): 259–70.

Loury, Glenn (1977). "A Dynamic Theory of Racial Income Differences." Pp. 153–88 in P.A. Wallace and A. LeMund (eds.), *Women, Minorities and Employment Discrimination*. Lexington, MA: Lexington Books.

Marsden, Peter V. (2005). "The Sociology of James Coleman." *Annual Review of Sociology* 31: 1–24.

Mouw, Ted (2006). "Estimating the Causal Effect of Social Capital: A Review of Recent Research." *Annual Review of Sociology* 32: 79–102.

Narayan, Deepa and Michael F. Cassidy (2001). "A Dimensional Approach to Measuring Social Capital: Development and Validation of a Social Capital Inventory." *Current Sociology* 49(2): 59–102.

Newton, Kenneth (2007). "Social and Political Trust." Pp. 343–66 in Russell J. Dalton and Hans-Dieter Klingemann (eds.), *The Oxford Handbook of Political Behavior*. New York: Oxford University Press.

Olson, Mancur (1965). *The Logic of Collective Action: Public Goods and the Theory of Groups*. Cambridge, MA: Harvard University Press.

Paxton, Pamela (1999). "Is Social Capital Declining in the United States? A Multiple Indicator Assessment." *American Journal of Sociology* 105(1): 88–127.

Paxton, Pamela (2002). "Social Capital and Democracy: An Interdependent Relationship." *American Sociological Review* 67(2): 254–77.

Portes, Alejandro (1998). "Social Capital: Its Origins and Applications in Modern Sociology." *Annual Review of Sociology* 22: 1–24.

Portes, Alejandro (2000). "The Two Meanings of Social Capital." *Sociological Forum* 15: 1–12.

Portes, Alejandro and Erik Vickstrom (2011). "Diversity, Social Capital and Cohesion." *Annual Review of Sociology* 37: 461–79.

Putnam, Robert D. (1993). "The Prosperous Community: Social Capital and Public Life." *The American Prospect* 4: 35–42.

Putnam, Robert D. (1994). "Social Capital and Public Affairs." *Bulletin of the American Academy of Arts and Sciences* 47(8): 5–19.

Putnam, Robert D. (1995a). "Tuning In, Tuning Out: The Strange Disappearance of Social Capital in America." *Political Science and Politics* 28(4): 664–83.

Putnam, Robert D. (1995b). "Bowling Alone: American's Declining Social Capital." *Journal of Democracy* 6: 65–78.

Putnam, Robert D. (2000). *Bowling Alone: The Collapse and Revival of American Community*. New York: Simon & Schuster.

Putnam, Robert D. (ed.) (2002). *Democracies in Flux: The Evolution of Social Capital in Contemporary Society*. Oxford: Oxford University Press.

Putnam, Robert D. (2007). "E Pluribus Unum: Diversity and Community in the Twenty-first Century." *Scandinavian Political Studies* 30(2): 137–74.

Putnam, Robert D. (2020). *The Upswing: How America Came Together a Century Ago and How WE Can Do It Again*. New York: Simon & Schuster.

Putnam, Robert D., R. Leonardi, and R. Nanetti (1993). *Making Democracy Work: Civic Traditions in Modern Italy*. Princeton, NJ: Princeton University Press.

Sabatini, Fabio (2009). "Social Capital as Social Networks: A New Framework for Measurement and an Empirical Analysis of Its Determinants and Consequences." *The Journal of Socio-Economics* 38(3): 429–42.

Sandefur, Rebecca L. and E.O. Laumann (1998). "A Paradigm for Social Capital." *Rationality and Society* 10(4): 481–501.

Schwadel, Philip and Michael Stout (2012). "Age, Period and Cohort Effects on Social Capital." *Social Forces* 91(1): 233–52.

Small, Mario L. (2009). *Unanticipated Gains: Origins of Network Inequality in Everyday Life*. New York: Oxford University Press.

Sobel, Joel (2002). "Can We Trust Social Capital?" *Journal of Economic Literature* 40(1): 139–54.

Solow, Robert M. (1995). "But Verify." *The New Republic* (September 11): 36–9.

Stolle, Dietlind (2007). "Social Capital." Pp. 655–74 in Russell J. Dalton and Hans-Dieter Klingemann (eds.), *The Oxford Handbook of Political Behavior*. Oxford: Oxford University Press.

Stolle, Dietlind and Marc Hooghe (2005). "Inaccurate, Exceptional, One-Sided or Irrelevant? The Debate about the Alleged Decline of Social Capital and Civic Engagement in Western Societies." *British Journal of Political Science* 35: 149–67.

Svendsen, Gert T. and Gunnar Lind Haase Svendsen (2009). *The Handbook of Social Capital: The Troika of Sociology, Political Science and Economics*. Cheltenham, UK and Northampton, MA, USA: Edward Elgar Publishing.

Thiess-Morse, Elizabeth and John R. Hibbing (2005). "Citizenship and Civic Engagement." *Annual Review of Political Science* 8 (June): 227–49.

Uslaner, Eric M. (2009). "Corruption." Pp. 127–42 in Gert T. Svendsen and Gunnar Lind Haase Svendsen (eds.), *The Handbook of Social Capital: The Troika of Sociology, Political Science and Economics*. Cheltenham, UK and Northampton, MA, USA: Edward Elgar Publishing.

Woolcock, Michael (2010). "The Rise and Routinization of Social Capital, 1988–2008." *Annual Review of Political Science* 13: 469–87.

2   Networks

> The *core idea* of social capital theory is that social networks have value.
> (Putnam 2000: 19)

The core concept in almost all definitions of social capital is the network of social relations in which actors are embedded.[1] For Nan Lin (2001: 56), "Social capital consists of resources embedded in one's network or associations ... resources accessible through direct and indirect ties." It is this network composed of our ties to one another that provides access to resources and information central to our daily lives that is typically referred to as the "capital" we obtain from our social connections.[2] Through these network ties we obtain word of new jobs, daycare openings, work, school, and cultural events, and more. We also gain access to resources of value such as lending tools and small appliances, borrowing bikes, sports or camping equipment for a weekend, getting or giving a ride, finding a place to stay, and even selling things no longer wanted and buying items currently desired. If network "ties" are important in terms of providing access or paths to resources of value, then characteristics of the network "nodes" which the ties connect are also important. What matters most is the nature and the number of resources they possess and their power and status within the various social settings they inhabit that open doors to resources and the kinds of information and influence valued by others. Networks are at the heart of social capital.

The global pandemic of 2020 and 2021 put in high relief the value of social connections and the network social capital they entail. In fact, the digital divide between those with easy access to connections online and those without became much more visible as a source of widespread inequality at the center of the ability of many to escape the ravages of the Covid-19 illness and its consequences. In addition to effects on the capacity to survive the epidemic and continue to engage in productive activities, networks became more central not only to our social and work lives, but also to our political activities. They also represent a significant channel of social influence. Long before the global pandemic the role of social networks and the social capital they provide had been identified as key to emerging social and political movements around the world.

Lin (2001), for example, was prescient in his discussion of the rise of social capital facilitated by cybernetworks across the globe. In his concluding chapter Lin analyzes the Falun Gong movement in China and how connections in cyberspace facilitated growth of the movement involving millions inside and outside of China. The Internet helped to sustain collective action on the part of the movement. The incidents Lin (2001: 225) examines serve as illustrations of "how social networks and capital provide the mechanisms and processes by which an alternative ideology, challenging prevailing ideology and institutions can be institutionalized." Many other social movements have been similarly organized through social media platforms and the social networks they foster. The Arab Spring, which began in 2010 and lasted for two years is another example. It included a number of uprisings and anti-government protests that were pro-democracy in countries in which citizens were tired of autocratic rule, poverty, and extreme inequality.

Fast forward a decade or so and this same set of mechanisms and pro-cesses involving the role of social networks fueled not pro-democratic, but anti-democratic movements in the United States during the second election cycle for the presidency of Donald J. Trump in 2020. Smaller anti-establishment, "right-wing" groups and militias were able to coa-lesce and mobilize to halt the confirmation proceedings of the Electoral College vote on January 6, 2021 for several hours. Members and affiliates of these groups stormed the United States Capitol and sent congressional members and staff into hiding. This capacity to mobilize, spread ideology, and foment collective actions against elected officials is an example of what some would refer to as the "dark side" of social capital. It can be put to various purposes, not all good. Even Putnam (1994) argued early on that social capital could be put to bad purposes. Nothing assures us that it will be put to good purposes.

Reactions to the killing of George Floyd, an African American, also fueled a social movement that engulfed many cities and communities prior to the January 6 events in Washington D.C. at the Capitol. This movement was stimulated not only by the Floyd murder but also by many other deaths of black victims at the hands of local police in various places in the United States and by the growing acknowledgment of the existence and persistence of structural racism in the society at large. Online activity fueled this movement as it expanded worldwide in a similar reckoning with race relations in several countries.

Most often, social media facilitated the coordination of protests as social networks provided information about events and content that stimulated angry reactions, particularly the circulation of videos that documented police brutality. The Black Lives Matter (BLM) movement grew to encompass many such events, building on earlier deaths attributed to law enforcement "overreach" and the unwarranted use of force. In such cases, networks provide "social capital" to those involved giving them important information and resources to pursue their causes, as well as the capacity to influence others who might join. There are many examples in history of such movements. Various aspects of networks determine who has access to valued resources in a wide range of contexts with differing consequences. Social movements represent only one domain of activity in which social capital network effects have been thoroughly investigated. In this chapter, we discuss network effects in several other domains indicating the breadth of their impact in society. Networks have even become the focus of an ever-expanding network science that cuts across many disciplines, moving beyond the social sciences (cf., Watts 2003) and rapidly becoming a focus of interdisciplinary research.[3]

2.1   Features of network location and social capital

Given that networks are one source of the "embedded resources" that represent one's social capital, as Lin (2002) has argued specific features of the network itself, as well as characteristics of the nodes in the network, matter. Bourdieu (1986: 248) originally focused on the "durable network of more or less institutionalized relationships of mutual acquaintance" linked to the "actual or potential resources" they make available to individuals. And, as Portes (1998: 3) points out, this conceptualization identifies at least two important elements: the social relationship itself and the amount and quality of the resources possessed by their associates.

Other researchers have also focused their attention on networks as sources of social capital. For example, Nahapiet and Ghoshal (1998: 243) define social capital, in line with Bourdieu (1986), as "the sum of the actual and potential resources embedded within, available through, and defined from the network of relationships possessed by an individual or social unit." And Durlauf and Fafchamps (2005: 1692) conclude that "the role of networks in facilitating exchange is one of the most compelling empirical findings in the social capital literature." Even in simple exchanges, networks are known to facilitate individuals finding one another to engage in exchanges that leave both better off. For Frey (2016) this means that when buyers and sellers, for instance, are part of a network that creates opportunities for information exchange, they are more likely to complete a transaction from which there are mutual gains even when contrasted with situations in which costly contracts diminish overall gains.

Lin developed an influential theory of social capital based primarily on a network approach. Key factors that affect one's access to social capital in his view are (1) one's *position* in a hierarchical structure, (2) the nature of one's *ties to others* in the network, and (3) the *location* of one's ties to others in the network (Lin 2001: 63). The hierarchies involved vary by culture but those at the top are typically argued to have greater access through either direct or indirect ties to others near the top with valuable resources. For Lin, these include wealth, power, and reputation, or what he refers to as economic, political, and social resources.

There are two broad sources of these embedded resources – network location and structural position – in Lin's (2001) theory of social capital. *Structural position* is the position one occupies in a hierarchy, particularly the pyramidal hierarchy he identifies as primarily the hierarchy of social positions in society, often determined by one's occupation or social structural position, or both. These hierarchies represent structures in which authority, rules, and positions are linked to locations in the hierarchy and thus access to resources made available at those locations.

But not everyone has equal access to the coveted positions in the networks in which they work. Access is structured, as it is in many walks of life, by one's broader position in society. An example that Lin (2000) explores is minority and gender status in the local society. He concludes from his research that both women and minorities have less robust access to social capital. Their networks are deficient in comparison to men's and to those with majority ethnic/racial status. In addition to more limited access, he reports that the "returns" on their social capital in the form of network ties that provide resources of value are lower. Thus, access to positions higher in the hierarchy is stratified and location is affected by one's social status as well as other factors relevant to occupancy in that system of network ties. Social inequalities persist in most cultures and differentially structure opportunity and access to network embedded resources. This fact was a key focus of early proponents of the use of the term social capital such as Loury (1977) and Bourdieu (1986). Putnam (2000) also emphasized differential access to networks as problematic given that, as he argued, social connections affect life chances. Network ties that are structured by social status and the connections it provides can make a difference in the capacity for those who grow up in areas in which their families are also rich in connections to find employment and to be more generally success-ful in their educational and occupational pursuits. "Those who grow up in socially isolated, rural and inner-city areas are held back, not merely because they tend to be financially deprived ... but also because they are relatively poor in social ties that can provide a 'hand up'" (Putnam 2000: 319).

As Lin (2001: 75) spells out in one of his theoretical postulates: "The higher the level in the hierarchy, the greater the concentration of valued resources, the fewer the number of positions, the greater the command of authority, and the smaller the number of occupants." A correlate of hierarchical location is typically status within the hierarchy; while derived from location it provides a particular set of resources including most notably prestige, authority, and control over information as well as material resources. Researchers have examined a wide range of effects of having such status on compensation and other factors correlated with status in an organization (cf. Belliveau, O'Reilly III, and Wade 1996). Positional status, when it enhances social similarity, is often associated with collaboration or alliance formation since similarity (or homophily) fosters connection formation (Chung, Singh, and Lee 2000). In addition, research indicates that "those at the top" of the status order in society typically have greater access to experts (York Cornwell and Cornwell 2008) than do others. Furthermore, these authors find that this disparity in access has increased over time in the United States, as it has in other countries plagued with inequality.

The other source of embedded resources is actual *network position* (independent of the status attached to it), which in Lin's view can be constrained by one's location in the relevant hierarchy. This means that those at the top and those at the bottom have fewer opportunities for "networking," while those in the mid-range of the hierarchy have greater opportunities to gain access to resources of value available to those both "above" and "below" them in the structure in which they are embedded. What matters in this theoretical approach to the analysis of social capital and where or how it is accessed is the opportunity structure and the limits or affordances it offers – in a word, *location*! Van der Gagg and Snijders (2005) developed an important survey instrument to measure access to resources available from the members of an individual's network. They identify four significant dimensions of such resources including political and financial capital, socio-economic status (SES)-related resources,[4] individual skill sets, and support in a study of the Dutch using a representative sample.

Important aspects of location, beyond centrality and closeness to those in positions of power, are the strength or weakness of the ties that emanate from one's position, as well as whether one is located near a bridge or not (or serves as a bridge to others in the network(s) with resources of value). And serving as a bridge often has advantages.

2.2   Bridging and bonding

An early proponent of a network perspective on social capital, Ron Burt (1992), developed a clear rationale for the impact of one key aspect of network location, the role of "structural holes" in the network and the connections that bridge across them. For him, "Participation in, and control of, information diffusion underlies the social capital of structural holes" (Burt 2001: 34). Burt's work on social capital emphasizes brokerage roles. Bridging across holes in a network creates opportunities for brokerage and thus provides a competitive advantage when the flow of information across network ties produces a valuable resource. For Burt, such bridges are most important when they link two clusters or subgroups that would have no connection at all if it weren't for the one actor with a bridging tie to another in a relevant group that provides valued resources (i.e., links to actors with higher positions in a hierarchy and thus greater access to valuable resources or simply links to those with the necessary resources wherever they are located in the network).

In Lin's network theory of social capital, just being close to a bridge increases one's access to social capital. As he notes (Lin 2001: 95), "Positions at or near strategic locations ... may provide a competitive advantage to actors accessing heterogeneous and thus rich resources." But it depends on the needs for and uses of these resources. Spanning sparsely linked network clusters facilitates the transfer of information and resources (Burt 1992, 2004). In empirical work on this topic in the domain of hiring decisions, for instance, Bills, Di Stasio, and Gerxhani (2017) document the fact that bridging or spanning network ties increase access to a diversity of information available to employers about potential employees and their qualifications or "fit" for specific positions. This facilitates hiring, making search more efficient.

Bridging ties also tend to connect people from more diverse backgrounds. In the domain of ethnic conflict, it is argued that ties that bridge groups in conflict with one another may create more peaceful avenues for conflict resolution since they bridge across group boundaries (Simmel [1908] 1955; Brewer and Miller 1984, 1996) and may broaden or redefine the existing boundaries. Stolle (2007: 660) notes in studies of conflict between Hindus and Muslim groups in India conducted by Varshney (2001) that "in cities where both communities have little social interaction, communal conflict periodically descends into violence" and riots. In such cases, cross-cutting ties that have the potential to bridge conflict and create the grounds for more positive intergroup relations are absent.

Rather than addressing conflict resolution possibilities, Burt (1992, 2001) stresses the strategic competitive advantage proffered by brokerage ties that span holes in the network. Others, however, suggest that these same ties can be problematic (see Stovel and Shaw 2012). Podolny and Baron (1997), for example, argue that boundary spanning, although advantageous for the transfer of resources and information, may be "harmful when spanning identities and expectations" resulting in ambiguity and the potential for split loyalties. They may also undermine trust. Podolny (2001) examines the "duality" of network ties and the gains or losses to the social capital that can be derived from these two types of ties, those that involve information and resources and those that involve important identities and expectations, including assessments of trustworthiness.

Despite the capacity to facilitate social interactions and enhance benefits in various realms, Stovel and Shaw (2012: 139) point out that it is also the case that "brokerage often breeds exploitation, the pursuit of personal profit, corruption, and the accumulation of power ... exacerbating inequalities." Others suggest further limitations of brokerage. Fernandez and Gould (1994: 1483) argue that "actors whose structural position bridges 'synapses' in a social network derive an advantage from this position only as long as they do not openly try to use this advantage." Impartiality of those occupying such positions is valued in some cases, especially when they serve as representatives of those they connect or as gatekeepers (see argument in Granovetter 2017: 110). If, instead, they are used to gain further advantages for the broker, those they connect may withdraw from the relationships involved. Or, as Granovetter (2017: 111) suggests: if the broker derives power from his central position in a structural hole "by keeping people apart rather than bringing them together, what is to prevent erosion of this power" by those "allying with one another to overcome the broker's advantage?" Emerson (1962, 1976) refers to this type of alliance formation appropriately as a power-balancing mechanism in networks.

Other network features, beyond structural holes, have consequences for the distribution of resources and their availability across the network of contacts in various settings. Density, for example, when it is associated with increased social cohesion, may lead to positive outcomes for those in the network often through the greater ease of resource and information flow. Alguezaui and Filieri (2010) investigate the role of social capital in innovation exploring the differential effects of sparse versus dense networks. They identify both knowledge search and sharing as activities that are central to creativity and innovation, noting that both occur more easily in dense or more cohesive networks. Similarly, Tsai and Ghoshal (1998) demonstrate the positive role of intrafirm networks, as a form of social capital, in value creation in business organizations. In further examining innovation and the role of network structure, Zaheer and Bell find that intrafirm networks, in their study of Canadian mutual fund companies, facilitate the exploitation of the firm's internal capabilities as well as their connections to other innovative firms. They point out that "innovative firms that also bridge structural holes get a performance boost, suggesting that firms need to develop network-enabled capabilities" (Zaheer and Bell 2005: 809), a finding that supports Burt's view of the utility of bridging ties, particularly those that span structural holes in interorganizational space as well as within firms. Under certain conditions, such ties facilitate success.

Many studies provide additional evidence of the benefits (and limitations) that network access has in the world of business, particularly in the domain of innovation. As is the case in many other domains of activity, including hiring, networks can provide new sources of information, increasing the diversity of inputs. Studies of problem-solving, for example, also emphasize the role of diverse information sources to enhance creativity and expand the range of solution options (Page 2017). Productivity is also linked to the diversity of teams when rates of interaction are high (Reagans and Zuckerman 2001).

Network density, however, can have negative consequences in communities in which local institutions are weak. In work on social capital and crime, for example, Morenoff, Sampson, and Raudenbush (2001) find that dense networks composed of strong ties may actually reinforce criminal tendencies and reduce the capacity for local social control. These findings reflect similar results found in existing research on areas in which Mafia organizations are strong (Gambetta 1988). Morenoff et al. (2001) conclude that networks and voluntary associations in neighborhoods lower homicide rates only when they facilitate general social control and support collective efficacy within the neighborhood rather than reinforce existing criminal activities. Strong ties in some contexts, thus, are to some extent a double-edged sword.

2.3   Ties that bind

An important distinction made in both Burt's (1992) work and that of Putnam (1995), which we have emphasized above, is the distinction between bridging and bonding ties. In fact, a small cottage industry has been examining the different roles of bridging and bonding ties in various aspects of social and economic life. Others have added "linking" as a separate type of tie, one that *links* actors to those in power or higher status, to those with political influence and financial resources. For Nan Lin these are the hierarchical ties identified in his theoretical approach. As Sabatini (2009: 275) argues, this kind of network (with linking ties) "is critical for leveraging resources, ideas and information ... that may play a significant role in social well-being." In this work he focuses on the integration of immigrants into European labor markets as a potential indicator of broader social integration. He demonstrates that such integration varies not only by access to social capital (in the form of network capital), but also by the nature of the state and the extent to which it is a welfare state providing important social and health services. In this section we focus primarily on the role of *bonding* ties.

Burt (2001: 35) discusses the network constraints that emerge from the nature of one's ties (bonding or bridging). And as Svendsen and Svendsen (2009: 5) point out, "different mechanisms are at work in bonding and bridging and they have different positive and negative implications" (see also Patulny and Svendsen 2007). Network ties not only offer access to resources of value they can also restrict such access. In fact, closed networks, of the kind that Coleman (1988) discusses in his work on social capital, facilitate bonding ties and the resulting social cohesion may have positive consequences for those in the network. Therefore, Coleman views small, closed networks in which members can monitor and sanction one another for abiding by the relevant norms and reciprocal obligations as a good thing. But they may also limit connections to those outside the network of "insiders" or group members. This can "lock-in" network occupants, especially if the norms of reciprocity and other obligations restrict them from taking up opportunities elsewhere.

This downside of immigrant bonding, for example, in ethnic enclaves has been discussed by Nee and Sanders (2001), among others. In addition, tightknit networks may have strong boundaries that form the basis for counter-normative activities in the larger context. Recall our earlier mention of Gambetta's (1988) work on the Mafia in which bonds among network members are intense and cohesion is strong as well as in-group trust, but out-group ties are quite weak and viewed with suspicion. Often these closed networks support and sustain illegal activities, as well as corruption. In this case the tight bonds between group members foster mutual trust and help to limit the risk of exposure or defection. Expulsion from the group for violation of this trust is swift and certain.

Bonding ties also have positive consequences under some circumstances. As is true of other forms of social capital they can have both positive and negative effects. On the positive side of the ledger for immigrants, for instance, close ties to those they know who have immigrated earlier to a specific location can provide entry into a new society, social support, and often financial opportunities that allow them to get their feet on the ground and begin to find lodging, work, and other critical resources.

This form of entry to the United States is referred to in the literature on immigration as "chain migration." Those who came before assist those originating from the same home communities, some with family ties (Palloni et al. 2001), as has been demonstrated in the long-term study of Mexican migration to the United States, referred to as the Mexican Migration Project (MMP) led by Jorge Durand and Douglas Massey (2004). (See Massey 1993 and Hagan 1998 for discussions of networks and migration.) The incorporation of immigrants into the host society is determined in part by their choice of location when they arrive. As Epstein (2009: 290) indicates: "Joining a bonding network will decrease the assimilation process and joining a bridging network will increase assimilation and the social capital of the migrants." Choice of location clearly makes a difference.

As Nee and Sanders (2001: 374) argue, "Ethnic ties assume such a central role in the incorporation of immigrants that this form of social capital is often more important than human and financial capital in shaping the trajectory of adaptation for many immigrants." The downside is that they may end up living for long periods of time in these enclaves without gaining access to potential opportunities in other locales, reinforcing the closed nature of the communities into which they immigrate and often forestalling any integration into the larger social context. Integration might offer access to increased human capital. Some (e.g., Banfield 1958) have argued that bonding ties are a source of backwardness as a result of these constraints. Svendsen and Svendsen (2009: 5) also suggest that the "more tightly structured and exclusive nature of bonding social capital" often leads to more negative outcomes.

Sabatini (2009: 273) argues instead that there has not been enough empirical investigation of bonding (as opposed to bridging) ties leading to an "underestimation of the possibility for strong family ties to act as a positive asset for the agents' strategies of survival and for the economy as a whole." Such ties may provide the support needed by those whose work is precarious due to low wages, minimal benefits, unpredictable hours, and little job security. It has also been argued that, in the face of autocratic and repressive regimes, people often segment their lives into smaller social networks of close personal contacts (Badescu and Uslaner 2003) that offer support and lower risk. Volker and Flap (2001) talk about the post-communist period in Eastern Europe, noting that such personal networks were viewed as a kind of shelter from state meddling in their private affairs (cited in Gesthuizen, van der Meer, and Scheepers 2008). Sabatini (2009) explores the broader effects at both the individual and the societal levels of bonding, bridging, and linking network ties, focusing on Italy. In other settings, results differ. In the Netherlands, for example, Lancee (2010) found that bridging networks were linked to higher levels of income and employment for immigrants, whereas bonding networks had no effect on economic outcomes. Clearly, results may differ under varying circumstances and cultural settings.

2.4   Networks and unequal access to resources

An important topic that threads its way through a number of discussions of the role of networks as social capital is the effects of unequal access to resources. Nan Lin talks about it in terms of positional and hierarchical factors within networks that structure access as we have described above. There are also community, regional, and national factors at work when speaking of sources of unequal access. Important work by sociologist Mario Small digs deeper into the world of those who live in low-income areas to find out what structures their access to the resources that are so critical to well-being in such settings. For example, in his book, *Unanticipated Gains: Origins of Network Inequality in Everyday Life* (Small 2009), he studies childcare centers in New York and Chicago to examine the role of personal, social, and organization ties in the lives of those who live in varying neighborhoods, some low-income and some not. How do they gain access to services they need to facilitate work and home life?

Small finds that it is not just personal social capital that matters, but also the interconnectedness of organizations, including non-profits, within communities. In this way, Chicago and New York differ, especially in high-poverty sectors, with greater access afforded those who live in New York and use specific childcare centers that are well connected to other social service agencies and related non-profits, yielding more resources to those living in poverty. As Small concludes (2009: 173), "The sources of these ties and the motivations ... involved in transferring resources across them, cannot be understood by resorting to the traditional concepts of social capital ... These ties exist in the realm of institutional arrangements, formal agreements, reciprocal exchanges, and cross-sector partnerships

… ." Ties at various levels make a difference in the personal, social, and organizational realms and all contribute to the extent to which those who most need the resources accessible through these ties obtain them. Others have noted the significance of community and organizational networks as well. Carpiano (2006), for example, finds that not only the networks involved, but the actual level of resources in the aggregate available to the community and to those with access to them makes a major difference. It is not only the nature of the ties that matter but what those ties offer to residents. Restrictions to access for some in the community is a source of the inequality that pervades network-based social capital in many settings.[5]

An important implication of this work is the caution to policymakers that the simple prescription to move those from high-poverty areas to places that are not ignores the extent to which in some regions such a move would sever access to the existing resources that have been generated over time by organizations committed to improving the conditions of those who live in these communities. (See also Mouw 2006 on problems of the estimates of the effects of programs like Moving to Opportunity (MTO), which offered vouchers to families in five cities to move to areas with lower poverty rates.) The resources available to families are deeply embedded in the community and interorganizational relations that are not easily or often transferable.

Networks matter in many ways and the ties that make a difference are not only personal and social connections, but the ties among the organizations (state and non-profit agencies together) in places where people live as well as find the childcare they need that enables them to work and provide for their families, in addition to connections to other resources (e.g., healthcare, new employment opportunities, after-school programs) critical for ameliorating the consequences of poverty. Probing the effects of organizational embeddedness, Small (2009: 191) argues, "will yield more powerful insights into contemporary social inequality." It also moves the discussion of network capital up a level from personal and social networks to connections beyond the individual. How organizations in the social service sector are linked sets the context for connections that are made for those in the organizations involved or with those whom they serve. We focus on network ties and health consequences next.

2.5   Networks and health

One arena in which bonding ties have been investigated for some time now and seem particularly useful is in the domain of health behaviors and healthcare. Social capital in the form of resources available from one's network is implicated in a number of ways in the well-being not only of individuals but of groups and communities. Much of this research focuses on social support networks in which bonding ties play a crucial role. It is clear that social support typically comes from members of one's close social circle including family members and friends, even friends of friends as many have come to find out during health crises. Access to information that is important may come from "weak" ties rather than "strong" ties in such cases, given the distribution of relevant informational resources especially when confronting rare conditions or diseases that are newly emerging for which the information network is sparse. A good example is the types of information that circulated early on during the global pandemic of 2020, much of it based on rumor rather than scientific facts. Misinformation about the origins of the virus as well as the nature of the vaccines, their side-effects and effectiveness, as well as possible cures, continue to circulate widely creating difficult circumstances for public health officials and those involved in treatment and prevention. It is not easy to counter such misinformation, especially when the networks involved are large, densely connected, and global in reach.

There are many studies of the role that the kind of social support obtainable as a resource from one's social network has in improving both physical and mental health. In fact, Putnam (2000) argued that social connectedness (as a form of social capital) was one of the most important factors in the case of health and well-being. Many cross-sectional studies report a "strong association between the size and quality of people's social networks and their health with people who are less socially isolated and more involved in social and civic activities tending to have better health (e.g., Baum et al. 2000; Veenstra 2000)" (Halpern 2005: 75). However, as Halpern notes in his book on social capital, it is not always clear what the causal direction is in studies of social networks and health. Does poor health lead one to become more socially isolated or does being socially isolated lead to poor health, as just one example of potential causality issues? Other issues in this research relate to bias in reporting mental health status (typically underestimated) and its relationship to network size and quality of social support.

In several decades of research, Nan Lin examines the links between stressors, social support, and well-being, focusing particularly on positive health and mental health outcomes. He defines social support in terms of access to instrumental and expressive (emotional) provisions supplied by communities, social networks, and what he calls "confiding partners" (e.g., Lin, Simeone, Ensel and Kuo 1979; Song 2004). In this work, Lin and his colleagues clarify the nature of social support and its subsequent effects on various health-related outcomes, including mental health conditions such as depression (Lin, Ye, and Ensel, 1999). Halpern (2005: 85–6) identifies pathways in which stress, network ties, and health outcomes are connected. These include lowered stress due to positive support with fewer negative consequences, in addition to gaining insights into better behavioral strategies to cope with stress from one's support network.

Zhang and Centola (2019), in their very useful review of studies of networks that support health behavior changes, find that online connections to others in similar situations often serve to provide important sources of relevant practical information and medical advice, in addition to emotional support. This information and influence vector is especially important when the health behaviors at stake are sensitive and are facilitated by the maintenance of anonymity (e.g., sexual health-related behaviors, HIV matters). These authors also write about other network effects in the domain of health behavior, including network interventions that may facilitate both the diffusion of significant sources of information or resources, as well as the stimulation of positive changes in health behaviors such as obtaining vaccinations and ceasing smoking. Using selected network ties to push out important information and nudges to engage in healthy behaviors and avoid unhealthy activities has become a key public health strategy. This is one reason the veracity of this information is critical.

Other researchers have identified various ways in which network-based social capital can be used to assist in organizational reforms. As an example, Scott and Hofmeyer (2007) discuss ways in which network approaches, including the social capital they entail, can aid in the transformation of primary healthcare systems in the delivery of integrated services, breaking down some of the walls that get created by specialization. In this case it is often the interorganizational ties that matter, although they may impact interpersonal relations, in some cases creating new paths of influence and access to relevant expertise.

A distinction is made in this research between individual-level social capital (access to network resources) and aggregate-level social capital (referring to the density of connections at the organizational, community, or state levels). Evidence indicates that, at the individual level, access to network ties that provide relevant resources including information has direct and indirect effects (mostly positive) on health outcomes, including mental health (e.g., De Silva, McKenzie, Harpham, and Huttly 2005). At the aggregate level, the effects of social capital are less clear. It has some positive effects on self-reported health, and it seems to mediate the connection between local disadvantage (e.g., income inequality) and health outcomes, even mortality rates (Kawachi, Kennedy, Lochner, and Prothrow-Stith 1997; Kawachi, Kennedy, and Glass 1999; but see also Pearce and Smith 2003), although in some studies of these effects, the measures of social capital vary making it hard to compare findings.

In fact, Halpern (2005: 95) argues that the effect of the community over and above that of the individual's own social capital (here meaning mainly the quality and amount of supportive network ties) is "generally estimated to be relatively modest" (see also Poortinga 2006 on the distinction between individual and collective resources and their related effects). This is partly due to the lack of relevant data at the meso level to make certain estimates of these effects as well as potential ecological fallacies. It is often hard to separate individual- and aggregate-level effects from the data that are available. This is what makes work by Small (2009) and others important since it attempts to distinguish interpersonal ties from interorganizational connections as well as identify the community resources that matter in different settings.

Network social capital, at various levels, certainly has significant implications, not only for physical and mental health, but also for aging, health communications, and disaster preparedness which affect health and well-being (see review by Kawachi, Subramanian, and Kim 2008). And we have only scratched the surface of the ways in which network social capital relates to the factors that determine the health of populations in various countries, all of which vary in significant ways including in level of economic development, state provision of social and health services, degree of inequality, and amount of political will to improve living conditions for the poor. How we look at social capital and which dimensions are examined affect the nature of the policy implications that can be derived from existing research on health effects and the healthcare sector (see Szreter and Woolcock 2004 for a comprehensive treatment of this topic). In the next section we move on to a focus on network social capital and employment opportunities.

2.6   Network social capital and markets for employment

Strong bonds may lead to network closure and the social cohesion it fosters may increase trust among those in the network. Closure, as we will discuss in other domains, may be associated with homophily since research indicates that two factors are often important in the selection of social partners: (1) proximity and (2) similarity (McPherson, Smith-Lovin, and Cook 2001). Thus, while drawing potential employees from these networks may increase confidence in their suitability for a particular job and trust in them due to homophily and overlapping ties within the network, it also limits the pool of potential applicants and most likely their diversity. Bills, Di Stasio, and Gerxhani (2017) find that broader cross-cutting (or bridging) network ties instead provide greater access to more applicants and increase the diversity of the available information about prospective employees. In teamwork settings within organizations, homophily can also limit the range of viewpoints and relevant skill sets, reducing the odds of developing innovative problem solutions (Page 2017). In many settings, access to diverse sources of information has been found to foster creativity.

These findings provide some support for the long-standing work of Granovetter (1983) and subsequent researchers who have demonstrated the "strength of weak ties" in employment markets indicating that, in general, more and better information about potential jobs is available from those to whom one has more distant and indirect ties than from those with whom one has strong, direct ties (e.g., Yakubovich 2005). One reason is that information available from those to whom one is "strongly" connected (for which homophily is often relevant) is more likely to be redundant. This is a clear demonstration of the effect of network location and the nature of ties producing "social capital" for the network occupants.

Information is certainly one of the most highly valued resources flowing in social networks, a trend that has grown exponentially in the age of the Internet and the pandemic-fueled move from face-to-face connections to computer-mediated interactions as the primary mode of communication and collaboration among colleagues. Even children have been subject to the vicissitudes of their networks and access to technology as their school lives have been transformed into hours and hours of computer-mediated sessions using programs such as Zoom, Google Classroom, Blackboard, and Microsoft Teams, among others.

Work by various researchers explores further the linkages between features of networks and employment opportunities as well as commitment and firm loyalty or longevity (e.g., Calvo-Armengol and Jackson 2004). Compensation has also been examined. Boxman, De Graaf, and Flap (1991), for example, investigate the wages of Dutch managers, comparing the effects of their human and social capital. They find support for the positive effect of network social capital in finding jobs, as predicted in Granovetter's original claim, as well as an interesting buffering effect such that high social capital can lower the impact of human capital returns over time, implying greater significance of social over human capital. It appears that having network connections provides job opportunities and serves as an important resource once employed.

In examining the role of social capital in education and employment outcomes in general, Mouw (2003) argues that network effects may be due to homophily (i.e., the fact that similar people tend to associate with one another) as much as with the resources associated with contacts or connections. That is, one's network contacts may be of similar status, and it is this factor that yields positive or negative outcomes for access to valuable opportunities, depending on the status level (see also Lin 1999 on the effects of status attainment and its link to network structure). The main methodological issue in this research is that since many people choose their own friends and those with whom they wish to associate, some of the network effects captured by studies of social capital may be due to the selection of whom to associate with as much as with actual "network" effects of resource access on outcomes like education and employment. The same set of issues concerning the importance of selection effects may arise in studies that focus on group or neighborhood effects since membership or where we locate may also be driven in large part by choice.

It should also be noted (with respect to the effects of types of contact) that findings in general are not always consistent across studies concerning the effects of "weak" ties as a source of employment opportunities. Sabatini (2009), for example, finds that weak ties do not have this effect in his Italian data. Instead, he finds that information may be diffused through weak ties, but that they "do not concretely help workers in their job search actions" (Sabatini 2009: 282). Rather, the stronger bonds, particularly with family and friends, serve to provide job placement assistance as a part of the strong familism that Banfield (1958) writes about in the regions of southern Italy where market institutions are weak. Culture and context matter.

Sabatini does find that these strong family bonds, however, do have a negative effect on the development of human capital, perhaps by limiting access to opportunities outside the circle of kinship and friend ties, an effect also noted above in our discussion of the ethnic enclaves studied by Nee and Sanders (2001). In other contexts, for instance with respect to immigrants from Mexico, Aguilera and Massey (2003) found that such ties to friends and relatives who have previously migrated to the host country (in this case, the U.S.A.) aid in linking new arrivals to job opportunities that grant access to formal employment and often to decent wages, even if longer-term effects are less positive with respect to human capital development. These chains of migration critically support adjustment to a new environment that can sometimes be hostile.

2.7   The role of networks as social capital in business relations

Personal ties (direct and indirect) not only assist in finding employment under certain conditions, but also form the basis of business relations in many settings. The formation of networks of trusted contacts is often viewed as essential in highly turbulent and uncertain political and economic environments. In such cases, networks offer the security needed to facilitate informal contracts and trade relations, not to mention access to significant resources. These networks of stable, regularized exchange relationships reduce transaction costs and segment the market, making it less risky and more predictable for those engaged in ongoing repeat transactions.

Versions of these networks exist in many economies at varying stages of development. Examples are widespread, particularly in Asian economies. To avoid market uncertainty, business relations are embedded in broad networks of long-standing social ties, sometimes based on kinship. Japanese keiretsu networks, for example, reduce risk, making interfirm relations more predictable (cf. Lincoln, Gerlach, and Takahashi 1992). They may, however, limit competition and restrict access to other opportunities over time. Burt, Opper, and Holm (2021) find that strong networks of Chinese CEOs create business success, although they limit cooperation outside their closed networks of trusted contacts. The key role of personal relations in networks has long been known and studied in various contexts (see Uzzi 1999 on social relations and access to financial capital in the United States, and Uzzi 1996 on embeddedness and the economic performance of organizations). We comment in Chapter 4 on the use of personal relations to form business connections in Russia which is rife with risk, uncertainty, and exploitation (even occasionally at the hands of one's closest ties). Closed networks of trusted contacts are very important in such highly uncertain, risk-laden environments, but they have their downside.

In Chinese society, as many have noted (e.g., Hamilton and Fei 1992; Fukuyama 1995), business relations are frequently so embedded in such networks of long-standing personal connections that they create overlapping networks of ties based on direct and indirect connections. These networks not only form the basis for business relations and thus social organization but also function as a mechanism of social control in which informal monitoring and sanctioning can occur, in line with Coleman's (1988) view of the significance of bounded networks. As Hamilton and Fei (1992: 28) argue, when one party in the network fails to perform, others in the network are implicated; thus, they are typically willing to act as third-party enforcers. This same process works to ensure the repayment of micro lending loans, such as that provided by the Grameen Bank (Yunus 1999).

Codes of conduct are deeply engrained in the culture of the group or society, and such norms involving behavioral expectations serve as the main source of informal social control. Mutual trust, while it may develop, is not required, given the effectiveness of this form of informal normatively based control. These codes of conduct vary by the type of tie and, in China, they are referred to as "guanxi" relations with differentiated expectations. Obligations are socially structured based on the nature of the connections involved (i.e., family, more distant kin, friend, person from same birthplace, stranger, etc.). It is not easy for "outsiders" to fully grasp the content of these behavioral expectations that undergird many business and social relations in China, making it difficult for many to do business there without insider information and training, or knowledgeable agents.

Connections are key to business success in many cultural contexts. In fact, kin-based networks are the main source of entrance into economic activity for many families in various settings. It is this familial-based trust that Fukuyama (1995) argues eventually limits the emergence of a more generalized social trust that he believes is the basis for broader economic development. We address this issue further in Chapter 4. The problem with familial-based networks of trust is that they often exclude others and may generate distrust of "outsiders." This factor limits contact with those who might expand economic activity and thus generate new sources of economic opportunities and subsequent growth. Creating these bright lines between insiders and outsiders can also fuel ethnic conflict (an argument related to Putnam's concerns about ethnic homogeneity and social cohesion, which we address in Chapter 4).

In the United States, a very large literature examines the role of networks in the world of business and innovation (e.g., Powell, Koput, and Smith-Doerr 1996). We have already cited some of this literature. For example, in a study of new technology firms, Yli-Renko, Autio, and Sapienza (2001) find that greater interaction between firms and their customers increases the availability of knowledge that is useful and can be exploited for market advantage. The notion of the embeddedness of such relations was addressed in an important article by Granovetter (1985), who argued that there is not a clear line between interpersonal and interorganizational ties. They overlap, and both have consequences for the organizations involved. In a general discussion of this topic, Sorenson and Rogan (2014) identify the complexities introduced by the fact that organizational ties are in fact connections between people; thus, they are vulnerable to the characteristics of those in the position of "connector" or broker, and the nature of their relationships. Who owns the resources at stake, and how those who broker access are connected, and to whom, make a difference in who controls the network social capital, or the resources produced by such ties.

Even the level of affect that characterizes the relationships that connect organizations to resources is a significant factor in the extent to which the dependence on specific parties can be managed (Seabright, Levinthal, and Fichman 1992). Boundary-spanning personnel (as the connectors are referred to) often gain power by maintaining control over the relations they broker. Many firms are thus sensitive to such power/dependence dynamics (Emerson 1962, 1976) and adopt strategies to mitigate them. (See Sorenson and Rogan, 2014, for a discussion of these strategies; an example is the rotation of personnel in such roles.) These authors conclude that "the conflation of an interpersonal relationship with an inter-organizational one raises thorny and complex questions about who owns that relationship – employee or employer – and consequently who can benefit from it" (Sorenson and Rogan 2014: 275). And similar dynamics occur in many types of organizations, including those in the non-profit sector. In many complex ways, organizations are dependent upon those they hire and the networks in which they are embedded. We move on in the next section to focus on network ties that are mediated through technology and their increasing importance.

2.8   Networks and cyberspace

At the dawn of the twenty-first century, one element of network dynamics that Putnam (2000) briefly indicated might counter the trend of declining social capital with its hypothesized negative effects on civil society is the rapid expansion of the Internet worldwide and its consequences for social, political, and economic outcomes. In his chapter on cybernetworks and the global village Nan Lin (2001) argues for more research on the formation and development of groups and associations that span the globe and enhance the emergence of social capital through network ties and the resources they proffer. Such research could "provide clues as to whether and how social capital may be outpacing personal (human) capital in significance and effect, and how civil society, instead of dying, may be expanding and becoming global" (Lin 2001: 239). Putnam seems to have underestimated the potential effects of the spread of the Internet and its consequences in providing far-reaching ties and access to embedded resources (as network-based social capital). Recent history has demonstrated that such resources, when obtainable, have been put to various purposes, yielding both positive and negative outcomes for those involved. In addition, it has become quite clear that access is unequal.

Early in the development of widespread interactions via the Internet it was assumed that technology of this form would open doors and provide access to information and resources previously unobtainable, leading the way to greater equality of access. In general, most observers of the growth of the Internet were optimistic that such access would have a democratizing effect across the board, particularly with respect to the spread of information and ideas, not to mention relevant resources and access to trade. Such optimism was to some extent short-lived as it became evident that in many domains access was limited to those who had the technology versus those that did not, subsequently referred to as the digital divide. Hence, in many ways, this global trend in the changing nature of social, political, and economic interactions mainly exacerbated rather than ameliorated existing inequalities (Lin 2001). This fact has only increased in relevance as awareness of the widening of the digital divide and its disparate impact has grown, particularly in education and work settings, and even more so during the pandemic. Recent work on artificial intelligence and its applications has highlighted ethical issues as well in the use of Internet-based technologies and the algorithms they are based on, raising additional concerns about fairness and equity, not just access.

While early writings about the role of the Internet in a global context were overly optimistic about its effects, the past two decades and the various challenges created by climate change,[6] political upheaval in different parts of the world, and pandemics have forced more people to rely on remote connections. These challenges have darkened the picture. Misinformation, for instance, flows as freely and rapidly as accurate information. Tweets and other posts online that foment insurrection and enhance the viral nature of the spread of "alternative" facts can add fuel to the flames of anti-climate change and anti-vaccination movements slowing progress toward solutions. Social media has exploded, and its impact is visible in many domains of activity, supporting negative as well as positive actions. Connections made on social media can be viewed as one form of networked social capital that provides easy access to information, though its veracity is often indeterminate. And such connections may foment activities that undermine as well as support democratic institutions and the values at their core, as anti-democratic movements have demonstrated recently in various parts of the world, including the

United States. Misinformation made readily available on social media and political polarization have also fueled the spread of the 2020 global pandemic (Covid-19) in the U.S.A. and elsewhere in the world, affecting vaccine distribution and take-up, as well as federal-, state-, and local-level feuds over mask mandates and social distancing, actions that have been proven to reduce the transmission of this deadly virus.

Everyday transactions and interactions between people as individuals and in groups or organizations have become more mediated by technology than ever before in human history. This trend is increasing exponentially as a variety of factors lead people to move to the online world for much of daily life, changing patterns of work, home life, consumption, and travel. Such broad effects have clearly been hastened by the global pandemic of 2020–21 and its aftermath. In many ways the most important element of social capital, as identified by most of those who have written about it, is the networks in which people are embedded that provide connections to valued resources, including services. In fact, networks are not only central to the provision of things we need both from other persons and from organizations and institutions, but almost as important is the access it grants to knowledge and various sources of information and influence. Efforts to validate these sources and verify the trust value of the information that is shared are gaining significance in the global fight to tamp down the spread of false knowledge and its consequences (including corruption and criminal activities), a task that is fraught with complexities at various levels.

In the midst of such sweeping social changes that impact all sectors of society, sometimes negatively, it is somewhat comforting to realize that often the core networks of which we are a part (that encompass family members, near and far, as well as friends, both close and distant) tend to remain resilient, as Fischer (2011) reminds us. Even if the ways in which we stay in touch have been altered, moving from phone calls and letters to email, text and Instagram, Fischer's (2011) analysis suggests that we are "still connected" to those we count as friends and family although relations with non-kin may now be easier to enter and maintain in the computer-mediated age of interaction.[7] His work indicates that this type of network social capital is far from declining in importance in our lives. We also seem to be good at engaging with more distant others in our networks for sharing information. In fact, Mario Small (2017) finds that, when facing difficulties, we often choose to talk with those we are weakly connected to rather than close friends and family members, with whom we typically have stronger ties, in part to avoid confronting unwanted expectations and related consequences, or to hide an inconvenient truth. In his view the social capital we obtain from our networks certainly includes those linked to us in more distant ways, especially when we face challenges. We might even confide in a stranger. These findings underscore the value of the many ways in which we are connected to others and the ways they are connected to others, including groups, organizations, and institutions in which their lives are embedded. This is certainly the core component of the concept of social capital. In the next chapter we move on to focus attention on the role that norms play in coordinating our actions and fostering engagement with the provision of collective goods.

Notes

1. Dasgupta (2003: 314) agrees, arguing that "social capital is most usefully viewed as a system of interpersonal networks."
2. Lin (2001: 56) also indicates an important corollary: "One implication of the use of social capital is its assumed obligation for reciprocity or compensation." We return to this topic in Chapter 3.
3. As Watts (2003: 27) argues in proposing that a new science of networks is emerging, "the particular manner in which individuals interact can have profound consequences for the sorts of new phenomena—from population genetics to global synchrony to political revolutions—that can emerge at the level of groups, systems, and populations." It is thus important to understand the networks formed by these many interactions and their effects.
4. SES is a common measure of the degree of stratification in a society.
5. In a study of poor families in Tanzania, Cleaver (2005) finds that those in chronic poverty may face conditions and constraints that make it difficult for them to even access social capital (in the form of relevant community networks that provide resources) given their chronic poor health and the ramifications of living in poverty.
6. In a study in Africa regarding social capital networks and climate change, Kehinde (2021) finds that participation in these networks significantly influenced decisions of farmers to adopt specific climate change adaptation strategies and to engage in mitigation efforts.
7. Though Putnam (2000: 411) in general understated the potential for the Internet to change the landscape of social media and its broad societal effects, he was somewhat optimistic that we could "find ways in which Internet technology can reinforce rather than supplant place-based, face-to-face, enduring social networks."

References

Aguilera, Michael B. and Douglas S. Massey (2003). "Social Capital and the Wages of Mexican Migrants: New Hypotheses and Tests." *Social Forces* 82(2): 671–701.

Alguezaui, S. and R. Filieri (2010). "Investigating the Role of Social Capital in Innovation: Sparse Versus Dense Networks." *Journal of Knowledge Management* 14(6): 891–909.

Badescu, G. and Eric M. Uslaner (eds.) (2003). *Social Capital and the Transition to Democracy*. London: Routledge.

Banfield, Edward C. (1958). *The Moral Basis of a Backward Society*. New York: Free Press.

Baum, F.E., R.A. Bush, C.C. Modra, C.J. Murray, E.M. Cox, K.M. Alexander, and R.C. Potter (2000). "Epidemiology of Participation: An Australian Community Study." *Journal of Epidemiology and Community Health* 54(6): 414–23.

Belliveau, Maura A., Charles A. O'Reilly III, and James B. Wade (1996). "Social Capital at the Top: Effects of Social Similarity and Status on CEO Compensation." *Academy of Management Journal* 39(6): 1568–93.

Bills, D.B., V. Di Stasio, and K. Gerxhani. (2017). "The Demand Side of Hiring: Employers in the Labor Market." *Annual Review of Sociology* 43: 291–310.

Bourdieu, Pierre (1986). "Forms of Capital." Pp. 24–58 in John G. Richardson (ed.), *Handbook of Theory and Research for the Sociology of Education*. New York: Greenwood Press.

Boxman, Ed A.W., Paul M. De Graaf, and Hendrick D. Flap (1991). "The Impact of Social and Human Capital on the Income Attainment of Dutch Managers." *Social Networks* 13(1): 51–73.

Brewer, Marilyn B. and N. Miller (1984). "Beyond the Contact Hypothesis: Theoretical Perspectives on Desegregation." Pp. 280–302 in N. Miller and M.B. Brewer (eds.), *Groups in Contact: The Psychology of Desegregation*. Orlando: Academic Press.

Brewer, Marilyn B. and N. Miller (1996). *Intergroup Relations*. Buckingham: Open University Press.

Burt, Ronald S. (1992). *Structural Holes: The Social Structure of Competition*. Cambridge, MA: Harvard University Press.

Burt, Ronald S. (2001). "Structural Holes versus Network Closure as Social Capital." Pp. 31–56 in Nan Lin, Karen Cook, and Ronald S. Burt (eds.), *Social Capital Theory and Research*. New York: Aldine De Gruyter.

Burt, Ronald S. (2004). "Structural Holes and Good Ideas." *American Journal of Sociology* 110(2): 349–99.

Burt, Ronald S., Sonja Opper, and Hakan J. Holm (2021). "Cooperation Beyond the Network." *Organization Science*: 1–23. http://doi.org/10.1287/orsc.2021.1460.

Calvo-Armengol, Antoni and Matthew O. Jackson (2004). "The Effects of Social Networks on Employment and Inequality." *American Economic Review* 94(3): 426–54.

Carpiano, Richard. M. (2006). "Toward a Neighborhood Resource-Based Theory of Social Capital for Health: Can Bourdieu and Sociology Help?" *Social Science & Medicine* 62: 165–75.

Chung, Seungwha (Andy), Harbir Singh, and Kyungmook Lee (2000). "Complementarity, Status Similarity, and Social Capital as Drivers of Alliance Formation." *Strategic Management Journal* 21(1): 1–22.

Cleaver, Frances (2005). "The Inequality of Social Capital and the Reproduction of Chronic Poverty." *World Development* 33(6): 893–906.

Coleman, James S. (1988). "Social Capital in the Creation of Human Capital." *American Journal of Sociology* 94: S95–S120.

Dasgupta, P. (2003). "Social Capital and Economic Performance: Analytics." Pp. 309–39 in E. Ostrom and T. Ahn (eds.), *Foundations of Social Capital.* Cheltenham, UK and Northampton, MA, USA: Edward Elgar Publishing.

De Silva, Mary J., Kwame McKenzie, Trudy Harpham, and Sharon R.A. Huttly (2005). "Social Capital and Mental Illness: A Systematic Review." *Journal of Epidemiology and Community Health* 59(8): 619–27.

Durand, Jorge and Douglas S. Massey (eds.) (2004). *Crossing the Border: Research from the Mexican Migration Project* (with Nadia Flores and Ruben Hernandez Leon). New York: Russell Sage Foundation.

Durlauf, Steven N. and Marcel Fafchamps (2005). "Social Capital." Pp. 1639–99 in Philippe Aghion and Steven N. Durlauf (eds.), *Handbook of Economic Growth.* Amsterdam: Elsevier.

Emerson, Richard M. (1962). "Power-Dependence Relations." *American Sociological Review* 27: 31–41.

Emerson, Richard M. (1976). "Social Exchange Theory." *Annual Review of Sociology* 2: 335–62.

Epstein, Gil S. (2009). "Locational Choice, Ethnicity and Assimilation." Pp. 289–302 in Gert Tinggaard Svendsen and Gunnar Lind Haase Svendsen (eds.), *Handbook of Social Capital: The Troika of Sociology, Political Science and Economics.* Cheltenham, UK and Northampton, MA, USA: Edward Elgar Publishing.

Fernandez, Roberto and Roger Gould (1994). "A Dilemma of State Power: Brokerage and Influence in the National Health Policy Domain." *American Journal of Sociology* 99: 1455–91.

Fischer, Claude S. (2011). *Still Connected: Family and Friends in America Since 1970.* New York: Russell Sage Foundation.

Frey, Vincenz (2016). *Network Formation and Trust.* Ridderkerk: Ridderprint BV.

Fukuyama, Francis (1995). *Trust: The Social Virtues and the Creation of Prosperity.* New York: Free Press.

Gambetta, Diego (1988). "Mafia: The Price of Distrust." Pp. 158–75 in Diego Gambetta (ed.), *Trust: Making and Breaking Cooperative Relations.* London: Basil Blackwell.

Gesthuizen, Maurice, Tom van der Meer, and Peer Scheepers (2008). "Ethnic Diversity and Social Capital in Europe: Tests of Putnam's Thesis in European Countries." *Scandinavian Political Studies* 32(2): 121–42.

Granovetter, Mark (1983). "The Strength of Weak Ties: A Network Theory Revisited." *Sociological Theory* 1: 201–33.

Granovetter, Mark (1985). "Economic Action and Social Structure: The Problem of Embeddedness." *American Journal of Sociology* 91: 481–510.

Granovetter, Mark. (2017). *Society and Economy: Framework and Principles.* Cambridge, MA: Harvard University Press.

Hagan, J. (1998). "Social Networks, Gender and Immigrant Settlement: Resource and Constraint." *American Sociological Review* 63(1): 55–67.

Halpern, David (2005). *Social Capital.* Cambridge: Polity Press.

Hamilton, Gary and Xiaotong Fei (1992). *From the Soil: The Foundation of Chinese Society.* Berkeley: University of California Press.

Kawachi, I., B.P. Kennedy, and R. Glass (1999). "Social Capital and Self-Rated Health: A Contextual Analysis." *American Journal of Public Health* 89(8): 1187–93.

Kawachi, I., B.P. Kennedy, K. Lochner, and D. Prothrow-Stith (1997). "Social Capital, Income Inequality, and Mortality." *American Journal of Public Health* 87(9): 1491–8.

Kawachi, I., S.V. Subramanian, and D. Kim (2008). "Social Capital and Health." Pp. 1–26 in I. Kawachi, S.V. Subramanian, and D. Kim (eds.), *Social Capital and Health.* New York: Springer.

Kehinde, Ayodeji Damilola (2021). "Impacts of Farmer's Participation in Social Capital Networks on Adoption of Climate Change Adaptation Strategies in Nigeria." International Conference of Agricultural Economics, August 17–31.

Lancee, Bram (2010). "The Economic Returns of Immigrants' Bonding and Bridging Social Capital: The Case of the Netherlands." *International Migration Review,* 44(1): 202–26.

Lin, Nan (1999). "Social Networks and Status Attainment." *Annual Review of Sociology* 25: 467–87.

Lin, Nan (2000). "Inequality in Social Capital." *Contemporary Sociology* 29(6): 785–95.

Lin, Nan (2001). *Social Capital: A Theory of Social Structure and Action.* Cambridge: Cambridge University Press.

Lin, Nan, Xiaolan Ye, and Walter M. Ensel (1999). "Social Support and Depressed Mood: A Structural Analysis." *Journal of Health and Social Behavior* 40(December): 344–59.

Lin, Nan, Ronald S. Simeone, Walter M. Ensel, and Wen Kuo (1979). "Social Support, Stressful Life Events, and Illness: A Model and an Empirical Test." *Journal of Health and Social Behavior* 20(June): 108–19.

Lincoln, James R., Michael Gerlach, and Peggy Takahashi (1992). "Keiretsu Networks in the Japanese Economy: A Dyad Analysis of Intercorporate Ties." *American Sociological Review* 57(5): 561–85.

Loury, Glenn (1977). "A Dynamic Theory of Racial Income Differences." Pp. 153–88 in P.A. Wallace and A. LeMund (eds.), *Women, Minorities and Employment Discrimination.* Lexington, MA: Lexington Books.

Massey, Douglas (1993). "Theories of International Migration." *Population Development Review* 19(3): 431–66.

McPherson, M., L. Smith-Lovin, and B. Cook (2001). "Birds of a Feather: Homophily in Social Networks." *Annual Review of Sociology* 27: 415–44.

Morenoff, Jeffrey D., Robert J. Sampson, and Stephen W. Raudenbush (2001). "Neighborhood Inequality, Collective Efficacy, and the Spatial Dynamics of Urban Violence." *Criminology* 39(3): 517–58.

Mouw, Ted (2003). "Social Capital and Finding a Job: Do Contacts Matter?" *American Sociological Review* 68(6): 868–98.

Mouw, Ted (2006). "Estimating the Causal Effect of Social Capital: A Review of Recent Research." *Annual Review of Sociology* 32: 79–102.

Nahapiet, J. and S. Ghoshal (1998). "Social Capital, Intellectual Capital, and the Organizational Advantage." *Academy of Management Review* 23(2): 242–66.

Nee, Victor and Jimy Sanders (2001). "Trust in Ethnic Ties: Social Capital and Immigrants." Pp. 374–92 in Karen S. Cook (ed.), *Trust in Society*. New York: Russell Sage Foundation.

Page, Scott E. (2017). *The Diversity Bonus: How Great Teams Pay Off in the Knowledge Economy*. Princeton, NJ: Princeton University Press.

Palloni, A., D. Massey, M. Ceballos, K. Espinosa, and M. Spittel (2001). "Social Capital and International Migration: A Test Using Information on Family Networks." *American Journal of Sociology* 106: 1262–98.

Patulny, R. and G.I.H. Svendsen (2007). "Exploring the Social Capital Grid: Bonding, Bridging, Qualitative, Quantitative." *International Journal of Sociology and Social Policy* 27(1/2): 12–51.

Pearce, Neil and George Davey Smith (2003). "Is Social Capital the Key to Inequalities in Health?" *American Journal of Public Health* 93(1): 122–9.

Podolny, Joel (2001). "Networks as the Pipes and Prisms of the Market." *American Journal of Sociology* 107(1): 33–60.

Podolny, Joel M. and James N. Baron (1997). "Resources and Relationships: Social Networks and Mobility in the Workplace." *American Sociological Review* 62(5): 673–93.

Poortinga, Wouter (2006). "Social Capital: An Individual or Collective Resource for Health?" *Social Science & Medicine* 62(2): 292–302.

Portes, Alejandro (1998). "Social Capital: Its Origins and Applications in Modern Sociology." *Annual Review of Sociology* 24: 1–24.

Powell, Walter W., K.W. Koput, and L. Smith-Doerr (1996). "Interorganizational Collaboration and the Locus of Innovation: Networks of Learning in Biotechnology." *Administrative Science Quarterly* 41: 116–45.

Putnam, Robert D. (1994). "Social Capital and Public Affairs." *Bulletin of the American Academy of Arts and Sciences* 47(May): 5–19.

Putnam, Robert D. (1995). "Bowling Alone: America's Declining Social Capital." *Journal of Democracy*, January: 65–78.

Putnam, Robert D. (2000). *Bowling Alone: The Collapse and Revival of American Community*. New York: Simon & Schuster.

Reagans, Ray and Ezra W. Zuckerman (2001). "Networks, Diversity and Productivity: The Social Capital of Corporate R & D Teams." *Organization Science* 12(4): 502–17.

Sabatini, Fabio (2009). "The Labour Market." Pp. 272–86 in Gert Tinggaard Svendsen and Gunnar Lind Haase Svendsen (eds.), *Handbook of Social Capital: The Troika of Sociology, Political Science and Economics*. Cheltenham, UK and Northampton, MA, USA: Edward Elgar Publishing.

Scott, Catherine and Anne Hofmeyer (2007). "Networks and Social Capital: A Relational Approach to Primary Healthcare Systems." *Health Research Policy and Systems* 5: 1–9.

Seabright, M.A., D.A. Levinthal, and M. Fichman (1992). "Role of Individual Attachments in the Dissolution of Interorganizational Relationships." *Academy of Management Journal* 35: 122–60.

Simmel, G. ([1908] 1955). *The Web of Group Affiliations*. Glencoe, IL: Free Press.

Small, Mario L. (2009). *Unanticipated Gains: Origins of Network Inequality in Everyday Life*. New York: Oxford University Press.

Small, Mario L. (2017). *Someone to Talk To*. Oxford: Oxford University Press.

Song, Lijun (2004). "Nan Lin and Social Support." Pp. 78–106 in Ronald S. Burt, Yanjie Bian, Lijun Song, and Nan Lin (eds.), *Social Capital, Social Support and Stratification*. Cheltenham, UK and Northampton, MA, USA: Edward Elgar Publishing.

Sorenson, Olav and Michelle Rogan (2014). "(When) Do Organizations Have Social Capital?" *Annual Review of Sociology* 40: 262–80.

Stolle, Dietlind (2007). "Social Capital." Pp. 655–74 in Russell J. Dalton and Hans-Dieter Klingemann (eds.), *The Oxford Handbook of Political Behavior*. Oxford: Oxford University Press.

Stovel, K. and L. Shaw (2012). "Brokerage." *Annual Review of Sociology* 38: 139–58.

Svendsen, Gert T. and Gunnar Lind Haase Svendsen (2009). *The Handbook of Social Capital: The Troika of Sociology, Political Science and Economics*. Cheltenham, UK and Northampton, MA, USA: Edward Elgar Publishing.

Szreter, Simon and Michael Woolcock (2004). "Health by Association? Social Capital, Social Theory, and the Political Economy of Public Health." *International Journal of Epidemiology* 33(4): 650–77.

Tsai, W. and S. Ghoshal (1998). "Social Capital and Value Creation: The Role of Intrafirm Networks." *Academy of Management Journal* 41(4): 464–75.

Uzzi, Brian (1996). "The Sources and Consequences of Embeddedness for the Economic Performance of Organizations: The Network Effect." *American Sociological Review* 61: 674–98.

Uzzi, Brian (1999). "Embeddedness in the Making of Financial Capital: How Social Relations and Networks Benefit Firms Seeking Financing." *American Sociological Review* 64(August): 481–505.

Van der Gagg, Martin and Tom A.B. Snijders (2005). "The Resource Generator: Social Capital Quantification with Concrete Items." *Social Networks* 27(1): 1–29.

Varshney, Ashutosh (2001). "Ethnic Conflict and Civil Society: India and Beyond." *World Politics* 53(April): 362–98.

Veenstra, G. (2000). "Social Capital, SES and Health: An Individual Level Analysis." *Social Science and Medicine* 50(5): 619–29.

Volker, B. and H. Flap (2001). "Weak Ties as a Liability: The Case of East Germany." *Rationality and Society* 13: 397–428.

Watts, Duncan (2003). *Six Degrees: The Science of a Connected Age*. New York: W.W. Norton.

Yakubovich, Valery (2005). "Weak Ties, Information and Influence: How Workers Find Jobs in a Local Russian Labor Market." *American Sociological Review* 70(3): 408–21.

Yli-Renko, Helena, Erkko Autio, and Harry J. Sapienza (2001). "Social Capital, Knowledge Acquisition, and Knowledge Exploitation in Young Technology-Based Firms." *Strategic Management Journal* 22(6–7): 587–613.

York Cornwell, Erin and Benjamin Cornwell (2008). "Access to Expertise as a Form of Social Capital: An Examination of Race and Class-Based Disparities in Network Ties to Experts." *Sociological Perspectives* 51(4): 853–76.

Yunus, Muhammad (1999). *Banker to the Poor: Micro-Lending and the Battle Against World Poverty*. New York: Public Affairs.

Zaheer, A. and G.G. Bell (2005). "Benefiting from Network Position: Firm Capabilities, Structural Holes, and Performance." *Strategic Management Journal* 26(9): 809–25.

Zhang, Jingwen and Damon Centola (2019). "Social Networks and Health: New Developments in Diffusion Online and Offline." *Annual Review of Sociology* 45: 91–109.

3   Norms

Social capital – that is, social networks and the associated *norms of reciprocity* – comes in many different shapes and sizes with many different uses.

(Putnam 2000: 21)

Why were norms included in Putnam's (2000) list of the key components of social capital? After all, norms have been studied extensively in sociology and the other social sciences since the earliest days of these disciplines (cf., Durkheim [1895] 1982) and they have been central to many explanations of social behavior for over a century. Here we will explore their role as social capital and their connections to the other dimensions of social capital identified by Putnam. With respect to networks (the subject of Chapter 2) and norms, he argues recently that "social networks are the visible sinew of community that undergird a valuable norm of generalized reciprocity" (Putnam 2020: 158). This specific norm fosters cooperation and collective action, seeds social trust, and helps make social order possible.

For conceptual clarity in this book, we will treat norms as distinct from the social capital that we discussed in Chapter 2, defined broadly as embedded resources in the social connections made in networks and the various associations of which we are a part. As background, we point out that a major difference between life in small, isolated communities and in large, complex societies is the "declining significance of groups into which one is born and the growing significance of reciprocated choices between erstwhile strangers for human relations" (Blau 2002: 346). This move over time from communal norms to networks of association (often open networks) is central to the emergence of modern complex societies, changing the very nature of the central problem of social order (Cook and Hardin 2001; Cook 2005) and significantly altering the role and effectiveness of norms.

In more urban settings, networks form that enable people to establish exchange relations and the social bases for collective action, as Fischer

(1982) points out in his comparative study of urban and small-town networks in two small California communities. While sub-communities may form in urban settings that may approximate small-town life (e.g., gated communities or ethnic enclaves), the more typical form of engagement is network based rather than group based. A caveat here is that in the age of increasing social connection via the Internet, some group-based interactions are quite salient even though they are often "thin" in terms of content or highly specialized in terms of activity (i.e., self-help groups or social groups with limited purpose). They differ from the groups formed by kinship and the close-knit groups of friends and neighbors that once formed the primary basis for connection and assistance within the community.

In modern life, people engage with one another through involvement in many, sometimes overlapping, social networks (or social circles). What differs in these settings is the nature of the ties and the networks in which they are embedded. In urban settings, networks tend to be more specialized, more numerous, more sparsely connected and less multiplex (i.e., covering more than one domain). One's networks may be quite separate, for example, with family, friend, and work networks having very little overlap. In contrast, in small communities in which networks are often overlapping, they may include work, friends, and neighbors all in one large, more densely connected network. Thus, relations are linked across domains and multiplex, meaning that they cover a wider range of activities (see Fischer 1982). Norms of reciprocity are more generalized in such communities, even though they may originate in specific networks where they are somewhat limited and restricted to those in one network (i.e., the friendship network), rather than applicable to all members of one's variety of networks. And it is these generalized norms that facilitate cooperation more easily in small communities than urban settings through norm enforcement by group sanctions.

Putnam focused specifically on one class of norms, *norms of generalized reciprocity*, that in his view supported civic actions and the provision of collective goods. Coleman emphasized the closure of networks (creating group boundaries) as a source of social capital. The reason is that closed networks, much like tight-knit groups or communities, enhance the *effectiveness of norms* since violations will be visible to some in the network and they can be sanctioned by those connected in the closed network composed of dense ties. For Coleman, like Putnam, one form of social capital is thus the presence of norms accompanied by effective sanctions.[1] These norms allow for "softer" social control mechanisms given that they are internalized over time and thus guide behavior without the overlay of external sanctioning systems or authorities. And reputations can circulate in such networks readily, often enhancing the effectiveness of softer sanctions. In larger, more sparsely connected networks, norms are much less effective and reputations may be local or restricted to specific domains of activity, thus less transferable. In fact, in such networks, reputations may not circulate across network boundaries, or they may be restricted to only one component of the network involved. This fact also makes it easier for actors to shed a negative reputation and recreate a new, perhaps more positive one in a different context.

Coleman (1987b: 153) views social norms as constituting social capital for the primary reason that when they come into existence, they allow those affected by externalities (i.e., effects on other parties) to gain some control of the relevant actions. This produces, in his words, a "socially efficient outcome, in the sense that the level and direction of the action is governed by all of its consequences." Without normative "control," conflicts of interest often exist with each party pursuing actions in their own best interest without taking into account the effects on others. Such norms constrain these actions under many circumstances. When social norms fail at this task, there may be recourse to governmental and formal institutions (e.g., legal, regulatory).

Network density, Coleman (1988) argued subsequently, not only facilitates the reinforcement of norms but, as a result, produces greater social control. Closure and density, as noted in Chapter 2, also contribute to social cohesion and solidarity within the network that serve as resources at the individual and the community levels. Beyond serving the purpose of sanctioning when needed, such networks may foster collective actions and other forms of cooperation. They support collective action on behalf of those in the closed network, not only because the free-rider problem (or the failure to participate) is "solved" by the capacity to sanction those who do not contribute, but also because of the existing normative pressures to comply simply as a member of the community represented by the closed network. These normative pressures can be intense and failure to abide by the relevant norms may lead to exclusion. Actions are more visible in these networks and information usually flows freely. These norms also support trustworthiness since those who abide by group norms can be trusted, although given that sanctions for the failure of trust are strong and often swift, the trust that forms may be what some have referred to as "thin" trust. The true test of trustworthiness comes when the sanctions are unavailable or ineffective. We discuss more fully the role of trust in collective action in Chapter 4.

In general, norms involve accepted conventions for appropriate behavior in a given context and they can change over time when behaviors shift to represent a new "normal," once new forms of behavior are accepted. Norms are a major class of what Posner (2000) calls "nonlegal mechanisms of cooperation." Often individuals learn what is appropriate in the process of socialization, either as children as they age and learn which behaviors are acceptable under various conditions or in differing situations. In this case the socializing agents are parents. Socialization also occurs when individuals join new groups or organizations, or move to a new country, and learn what the accepted standards of behavior are in those settings. But sole reliance on the effectiveness of socialization is rare in most organizations.

Groups and other forms of association tend to adopt prescriptions (and proscriptions) for accepted (and unacceptable) behavior in part because norms can become internalized and, as a result, the need for external mechanisms of social control is reduced. But norms need to be reinforced and deviations sanctioned, either by various types of disapproval or by direct negative behavioral consequences. Abiding by the relevant norms of a group, social association, closed network, or community is frequently understood as the essential indicator of membership, defining who is in the group and who is not, reinforcing boundaries. As we discuss in Chapter 4 on trust, abiding by normative standards, much like mutual trust, also reduces transaction costs by lowering the need for monitoring and sanctioning systems and other mechanisms of external social control that can be costly. These costs are minimized to the extent that the norms are internalized as standards of appropriate action.

3.1   Norms of reciprocity

In discussions of social capital (as networks, norms, and trust), one aspect that is emphasized by Putnam (2000) is the presence of a specific set of norms: norms of reciprocity that facilitate social exchange between individuals and collective actions more generally (Gouldner 1960). Dense networks of association "entail repeated exchanges of what Putnam calls 'short-term altruism' and 'long-term self-interest': I help you now in the expectation that you will help me in the future" (Cohen 1999: 219). Cohen continues: "These rational exchanges and the direct experience of reliability, repeated over time, encourage the development of a norm of reciprocity."

Such norms are viewed by many social scientists in various fields as fundamental to social action and are found in almost all societies. Evidence comes from work on evolution and, more recently, neuroscience (de Waal 2003; McCabe 2003). Reciprocal exchange is even found in other species. As de Waal (2003: 129) puts it: "reciprocal exchange may have evolved in many animals (including humans) for similar reasons yet be achieved in variable ways." In fact, reciprocity may be more complex in humans and more dependent on the nature of the underlying relationship, the level of interdependence, and the capacity for what de Waal calls individual recognition, the ability to identify the specific other involved in mutual altruism or reciprocal exchange over time. Without such recognition, reciprocity is much less likely.

Ostrom (2003: 42) writes that "the specific reciprocity norms that individuals learn vary from culture to culture and, within a broad cultural milieu, across different types of situations that are confronted repeatedly." Social scientists have documented the fact that reciprocity norms exist in all cultures that have been studied. This norm specifies the obligation to return any favor or related positive action such as gift giving, doing something nice for someone else, or taking turns, for example, in paying the bill for drinks or dinner. It also may dictate responding in kind to negative actions. Within other species, especially those most like us genetically such as chimpanzees, reciprocity may involve turn taking, sharing, and mutual grooming, among other behaviors that have been investigated (e.g., de Waal 1989, 2000). As Ostrom (2000: 153) notes in a review of evidence: "... recent developments in evolutionary theory – including the study of cultural evolution – have begun to provide genetic and adaptive underpinnings for the propensity to cooperate based on the development and growth of social norms."

Theories of social exchange in sociology as well as anthropology have long viewed reciprocity norms as central to systems of dyadic and generalized exchange in societies ranging from early hunter-gatherer cultures to more modern cultures spread across the globe. As Cook (2005: 7) notes, "the distinguishing feature of social exchange is the uncertainty that surrounds it and the fact that one party can initiate an exchange with an offer of a gift, advice, or some other service without knowing whether and to what extent that action will be reciprocated." For Blau (2002), not only is expected reciprocity the bedrock of social life in general, but it also undergirds larger-scale social exchange, where trust in others is essential if there are no formal agreements between the parties involved and normative constraints are less effective.

A theory of reciprocity in social exchange, identifying the conditions under which we reciprocate acts of "giving" in exchanges with others in our society was developed by Molm (2010). Such norms often undergird cooperation and provide support for collective actions that benefit not only the individuals involved but also the network or community in which they are embedded. Whitman (2021: 528) notes that the norm of generalized reciprocity, when it is strong, fuels acts of generosity, both factors she identifies as "essential to networks of social capital." She goes on to argue that these "small acts of giving" can help to generate micro social order (Lawler, Thye, and Yoon 2008), "strengthening social bonds and the sense of community," including facilitating collective action. In fact, Cook, Hardin, and Levi (2005: 93) argue that communal norms could have grown out of reciprocal exchange relations within such groups. A communal norm of cooperativeness might arise out of these reciprocal exchange relations and then be transformed into a more generalized norm, though still potentially reinforced as a within-group norm. And they may be enforced by norms of exclusion such that violators are shunned or actively excluded from the group or network of social relations.

Some argue that the norm of reciprocity applies to negative behaviors compelling those who are harmed to react in a similar fashion creating a kind of sanction against engaging in behaviors that have negative consequences. But there is less evidence of this kind of negative "tit for tat" behavior in part because it can lead to a downward spiral and potentially the escalation of harmful behaviors. Molm (1997) discusses the downside of negative rewards or sanctioning and how individuals are less likely to use punishment power than rewarding power. An important correlate of the use of punishment power, particularly if not viewed as fair, is the possible termination of the relationship. McCabe (2003) finds some evidence of both positive and negative reciprocity in his work developing a cognitive theory of reciprocal exchange. He also finds neural correlates of reciprocity, indicating a deep encoding of this form of social activity that supports cooperation. And it is this support of cooperation that is viewed as fundamental to the development and maintenance of social order.

While norms have been studied as a key element of social order for many decades there is less clarity about when and how these norms emerge. Few accounts exist that spell out when behavioral regularities, for example, become accepted norms that carry force. Some accounts are based on an older functionalist logic that they emerge when they meet the needs of the individuals (or subgroup) involved, improving their welfare. (On the instrumentality of norms, see Hechter and Opp 2001.) But actors' interests may not converge and, in fact, may differ significantly as is the case with those who want to ban smoking in all public places and those who smoke who do not, for instance. Hechter and Opp (2001: 398) conclude that "It is far from obvious what individuals ought to do if they seek to establish a specific norm, and the members of groups usually have conflicting interests when it comes to many norms." So, consensus is far from assured. This is certainly the case with behaviors that might mitigate climate change as another example. There is continuing debate in many sectors over even the basic premise that climate change is occurring, though under the current circumstances that is hard to understand. Factors relevant to the formation (and change in) norms include social networks, culture, power, and politics, to name a few.

Legal scholars are interested in the evolution of social norms, since in many cases such norms become encoded in law to ensure that they continue to carry force in society, particularly when norms that protect others from harm weaken. And norm change is one of the many ways in which laws evolve and change over time as customs shift to accommodate new conditions in society, including the incorporation of immigrants whose customs vary. In one treatment of the value of analyzing norm emergence and change, building on the law and economics tradition, Ellickson (2001) argues that both demand- and supply-side factors are relevant. Change agents are invested in altering the existing norms to meet new conditions that revise the relevant costs and benefits of specific behaviors for particular groups. By his account, such agents include self-motivated leaders, norm entrepreneurs who stand to gain from the change, and opinion leaders who endorse change. The "social audience" includes those who support efforts to revise the existing norms or impose new ones, hence providing the "demand" for norm change.

Central to the process, according to Ellickson (2001: 51), is a kind of "exogenous shock—a shift in internal cost-benefit conditions or an alteration of group membership," both of which change the underlying value of the existing norms and spur a change in informal rules. It is a complicated calculus but one that is worth understanding if we are to account for norm change and the emergence of new guidelines for behavior as ever-present changing social and political conditions require. This discussion is relevant to the norms that arise in support of collective actions that provide for public goods.

3.2   The emergence of norms that support collective action

An important positive role for norms, as identified by Putnam in his work on social capital, is their role in promoting cooperation broadly and specific forms of collective action, such as the provision of public goods. They also play a role in fostering civic actions, a major concern for Putnam at the close of the twentieth century as a key part of his argument concerning what he viewed as the alarming decline in social capital. A long tradition of work in economics and, to some extent, sociology and political science focuses on the provision of public goods and solutions to the problem of free-riding that pervades such efforts.

A standard approach to this problem is to conduct experimental work using the prisoner's dilemma and related games to analyze the conditions under which cooperation occurs (see Cook and Cooper 2003 for a review) and the extent to which trust is a correlate of cooperation. In Chapter 4, we review Ostrom's general model of collective action and the key role of trust. Here we mention factors related to norms and what she calls institutions or rules of action in which solutions to public goods provision can be found and that link to the existence of trust. Ostrom (2000: 143) concludes that "recent developments in evolutionary theory and supporting empirical research provide strong support for the assumption that modern humans have inherited a propensity to learn social norms" which vary across cultures and situations. These norms define what is expected and prohibited in terms of appropriate behavior, violations of which typically result in guilt or shame, not to mention social disapproval and sometimes exclusion from the group. A distinction is often made between internalized norms for which non-conformity results in guilt or shame, and shared norms the violation of which is sanctioned by the relevant group members (Coleman 1987a; see also Ostrom 1990: 206).

Other factors that facilitate collective action include mechanisms that support generalized exchange (Simpson et al. 2018). Gratitude for acts of generosity (receiving help when needed) or concern for maintaining a reputation for being generous (and thus deserving of assistance when needed) are both reasons that generalized exchange systems, based on forms of reciprocity, emerge and are sustained. Referred to as generalized reciprocity and indirect reciprocity, both are relevant in explaining action that helps limit free-riding and counteracts the prominence of self-interest over the interest of the collective. These mechanisms include not just prosocial or altruistic orientations that may vary across populations but also strategic elements (concern for receiving aid and for maintaining a reputation) that support giving aid or contributing what you can. When norms are weak these factors become more significant. Often norms alone will simply not do the work required to counteract the tug of self-interest and free-riding.

However, both experimental research and field studies support the notion that, over time, rules or norms often do emerge that induce cooperation among individuals who stand to gain from the provision of public goods, such as water for irrigation, access to grazing grounds for animals to survive, building bridges and roads that facilitate access, and related resources that typically cannot be provided without collaboration. This research demonstrates that individuals can work together for collective gain more so than Olson's (1965) well-known book, *The Logic of Collective Action*, would have us believe. In this book Olson lays out the key reasons why it is that cooperation for common good often fails to occur, the primary reason being the likelihood of free-riding.

In discussing solutions to this problem, Olson suggests the need for selective private goods as one type of incentive for participation. Examples include the small gifts or tokens of appreciation provided to those who contribute to the continuing cost of public TV or radio, as well as setting up memberships with annual dues to provide ongoing support. As we have noted in our discussion of networks (Chapter 2), often what is fundamental to collective actions of mutual benefit is defining the boundaries of those who have access and those who do not, when that is possible. In this way those who fail to abide by existing norms and contribute can be sanctioned by denial of access to resources of value. But this is not always possible, especially when exclusion from consumption (as with public radio) or limitations on access (as with a local bridge that connects homes to a mainland, for example) cannot be implemented. In some cases, taxes on public goods are imposed by local authorities or providers to cover the cost, which solves the free-rider problem administratively. But this solution requires collective action at another level to support taxation.

3.3   The weakness of sanctioning systems

In various cultures when social norms of reciprocity are weak, external mechanisms are developed to sanction non-contributors but these systems themselves often fall prey to free-riding with the refusal of some to participate in the establishment of such mechanisms. That is, a separate collective action problem arises in the actual enforcement of the relevant norms of cooperation. This difficulty is typically called the "second-order" free-rider problem. Who will contribute to setting up a sanctioning system? This is also a public good. Fehr and Gaechter (2000) provide some experimental evidence that individuals do punish those who violate reciprocity norms (at least more than would be predicted on the basis of "rational" free-riding), suggesting that some of the time actors do contribute to sanctioning those who don't follow the relevant norms. What makes Ostrom's (e.g., 1990, 2000) work so influential in the policy world is that she provides evidence of the many ways in which collective action problems are solved around the globe and she documents how common features emerge even though they vary by culture and over time. This is the work that won her the Nobel Prize.

Another important, but troubling, finding in this broad field of research on collective action and the provision of public goods is the fact that external sanctioning systems may undermine the very incentives to cooperate that they are meant to enforce (see Mulder, Van Dijk, De Cremer and Wilke 2006; Simpson and Willer 2015). Given external constraints that impel cooperation and/or contributions, the internal motivation to do so may decline (Frey 1994) creating a kind of "catch-22" in which cooperative behavior is "crowded out" by the existence of external rules and monitoring systems. In addition, Ostrom (2000) concludes that, ironically, social norms in settings in which there is communication between the parties involved can generate cooperative behavior as easily as in settings with monitoring and sanctioning which are clearly more costly. She indicates (Ostrom 2000: 147) that these communally derived norms may have a "certain *staying power* in encouraging a growth of the desire for cooperative behavior over time." Such behavior induced by monitoring and sanctioning, in contrast, may be short-lived. What remains unclear is how these social norms evolve in the first place.

The same argument concerning "crowding out" norms of cooperativeness and the internal motivation to contribute is made about contracts. Specifying the terms of a contract down to the minutest detail may reduce trust since it signals a lack of trust undermining internal motivations to fulfill the contract (e.g., Malhotra and Murnighan 2002). Too much focus in organizational settings on monitoring and sanctioning for failure to abide by accepted standards of behavior (i.e., norms) has been shown to lead to "resentment and retaliatory behavior" (e.g., Cialdini 1996, referenced in Cohen and Isaac 2021: 189). Scholars have argued instead that taking a trusting stance initially in many settings, until proven wrong, may in fact induce trustworthiness. This approach has been shown to have some positive consequences in social service agencies (e.g., Braithwaite 1998) where monitoring and sanctioning is costly and has negative behavioral consequences in part because it clearly signals a lack of trust. In a more recent experimental study focused on this issue, Cohen and Isaac (2021) report that not only does trust beget trustworthiness, but also that it may trigger trust in others, outside the dyad, an important side benefit. Whether or not this also happens outside the social science laboratory, and when, requires additional research.

3.4   What works?

In field work in which collective action problems relating to common pool resource issues have been examined on the ground in places like East Asia, India, Africa and the United States, a number of factors have been identified that support solutions, often sustained over generations in some cultures. Strong leadership and effective communication are typically cited as significant factors in successful collective actions (Simpson and Willer 2015).[2] Ostrom (2000: 151) summarizes what she calls important design principles for such solutions: "When the users of a resource design their own rules that are enforced by local users or accountable to them using graduated sanctions that define who has rights to withdraw from the resource and that effectively assign costs proportionate to benefits, collective action and monitoring problems are solved in a reinforcing manner (Agrawal, 1999)." And it is the norms that emerge to support these solutions that help sustain them, often over decades. Related research (e.g., Sutter, Haigner, and Kocher 2010) provides additional support for the proposition that these norms (or rules of behavior) when developed by the groups involved, and not imposed on the group by local authorities, are more effective and sustainable (see Simpson and Willer 2015 for elaboration of this point).

The rules of engagement encoded in norms, when honored, are key to successful management of these important community resources. Examples include shared irrigation systems, common grazing lands, allocation of fishing rights, shared water sources, and even micro-lending loan circles. Economic development in many parts of the world relies on the proper management of these, often critical, resources. Another significant component of proper management is the capacity for conflict resolution. Given that conflicts are likely to emerge in many common resource settings, finding a mechanism for resolving them in ways that facilitate continued cooperation is critical. Community-derived solutions are preferable to the imposition of external forces since they are more likely to be effective. In fact, Ostrom (2000) reports in her field work that the self-organizing efforts by users of common resource pools to develop management tools, rules, and norms are preferable to those that are externally imposed, and they lead to more positive outcomes in terms of restricting overuse and supporting sustainability over time.

Ostrom (1990: 69) cites the work of McKean on Japanese fishing villages in which she analyzes the management of the common forest and farming lands, as well as the fishing supply, noting how the villages developed their own rules of use. McKean (1986: 571) argues that the success of these locally developed rule systems indicates that "it is not necessary for regulation of the commons to be imposed coercively from the outside." In fact, if there were too many violations, the village appointed their own "detectives" to identify the violators and the community developed its own price, often in sake to drink or donations to the village school (see Ostrom's long description of this case, among others).

A key factor in these situations is the degree to which the relevant norms apply to those engaged in the common resource activity (e.g., fishing when there is a limited supply and overfishing would be devasting for the local community). When those engaged in the activity are not part of the local community, normative control is weakened. In the fishing villages Ostrom (1990: 206) writes about, she notes that the trawlers that move in to take fish away from the small-boat fishers are often not part of the local community. As she notes, "they do not drink in the same bars, their families do not live in the nearby fishing villages, and they are not involved in the network of relationships that depend on the establishment of a reputation for keeping promises and accepting the norms of the local community." This sets the stage for conflict between the "locals" and the "outsiders." In common pool resource settings (or what Ostrom calls "CPRs") extensive norms develop to constrain overuse of the relevant resources. Especially when populations are fairly stable, outsiders rare, and resources are passed from generation to generation, Ostrom (1990: 88) indicates that such norms "make it feasible for individuals to live in close interdependence without excessive conflict." In the settings in which long-term cooperation for the collective good exists, it appears that norms alone are not wholly sufficient even though they are very important. Villagers, for example, do invest in some version of a monitoring and sanctioning system to assure survival of the critical resources at stake.

It is clear, initially at least, that the core norm involved in many of these settings in which cooperation or collective action of this type is required is one of reciprocity. Other relevant norms include those that focus on fairness and trustworthiness (for more on this topic, see Chapter 4). When those Ostrom calls "conditional cooperators" initially reciprocate a cooperative action and continue to do so when others cooperate, a solution to the underlying collective action problem may arise, especially when some of those involved are willing to sanction violators of the relevant norms. Ostrom (2000) refers to these individuals as the "willing punishers." Their role is significant since without them there would not be an easy solution to what is known as the "second-order" collective action problem noted above. What varies in this scenario is the proportion of individuals in a setting that act as "willing punishers" and the extent to which their actions facilitate contributions to the public good.

An important distinction is made in the literature between injunctive and descriptive norms. And much of the work on the role of norms in collective action focuses on injunctive norms (those that imply an "oughtness," often due to the sanctions entailed). Irwin and Simpson (2013), however, argue that too little research has been done on the role of purely descriptive norms that clarify behavioral expectations. If you find out that most others in your community, for instance, are conserving electricity, water, or fuel when it is scarce, what effect will this descriptive information have on your own consumption patterns? There is research to suggest that this information alone can make a difference under certain conditions. In their work, Irwin and Simpson (2013: 1057) find that "descriptive norms generate social identification (i.e., a sense of 'we-ness'), which then sustains conformity to expectations," whether it be expectations of cooperation or non-cooperation. That is, such information may support either success or the failure to provide collective action based on the nature of the content provided concerning similar behavior of relevant others (i.e., either cooperative or non-cooperative). The importance of peer enforcement of appropriate behavior and the role of moral judgments of others in supporting collective action (in contrast to material sanctions) is understudied, as Simpson, Willer, and Harrell (2017) demonstrate in their research on cooperation. Such actions also reinforce group boundaries, adding to the factors that help to produce effective collective action.

The significance of social identification (i.e., group belonging) is that it leads to social connections that reinforce group or collective interests. It can, however, lead to lower levels of contributions if the existing norms are non-cooperative, and even the most generous individuals in such situations often fail to contribute (see results from Irwin and Simpson 2013). Descriptive norms have a clear impact, either increasing or decreasing collective action based on the behavioral expectations encoded in them. As this work demonstrates, not all collective actions have positive consequences for those involved in efforts to provide or protect common resources and some actions may even undermine potential solutions.

3.5   Norms and the dark side of social capital

Norms, as we have argued, are most effective in small groups and communities that are tight-knit. Such groups often have clear boundaries that help define who is "in" and who is "out" of the group. As we have suggested, norms are basically agreed-upon "rules" of behavior or accepted ways of doing things. In addition, these groups or small communities usually accept the duty to sanction either, informally or formally, violations of the relevant norms. These norms can involve a wide range of accepted behaviors depending on the nature of the group. Families, friend groups, teams, clubs, gangs, militia, and online communities that can police membership all have the capacity to determine the bounds of acceptable behavior within the confines of the group and specify the nature of the sanctions for failing to meet group standards. These group norms may represent activities that fail to meet broader standards of behavior embedded in the larger community and thus they can undermine social cohesion at the community level. In fact, as Halpern (2005: 136) notes, "when pro-social relationships are weak, negative forms of social capital may fill the void, such as juvenile gangs, binding the individual into an alternative and competing set of norms and loyalties."

One good example of norms that can reinforce negative behaviors is norms that support corruption and illegal behavior (Uslaner 2009). Graeff (2009: 150) argues that in the absence of mutual trust, based on knowledge gained from past interactions, norms can regulate corrupt deals "if those norms clearly define what a corruptly behaving actor should do" and provide support for the presumed reciprocity based on an accepted norm among the actors involved in the completion of an illegal exchange. We discuss the conditions under which mutual trust emerges and can encourage such behavior as Gambetta (1993), Varese (2004), and others have demonstrated in work on the Mafia in Italy, in Chapter 4. In such settings, norms are enforced by the group and reactions to norm violations can be severe. Exclusion from the group (or worse) is often a consequence, even for kin.

Other examples of the power of norms to support negative behaviors in various groups abound in the literature on groups, gangs, and neighborhoods. Since norms are accepted standards of behavior there is no requirement that the norms specify that the behavior called for is ethical in a broader sense or that it be based on justice considerations. In some urban neighborhoods, plagued by violence and disadvantage, gangs may take hold of the streets and even require acts of violence, such as killing enemy gang members, as a kind of "initiation" into the group, demonstrating commitment and loyalty. It is this type of activity that is referred to in the literature as an example of the dark side of social capital, in this case related to norms of engagement in initiation rituals (leading in some cases to illegal behavior) and group inclusion, that often come at a high price. Norms of reciprocity also undergird this kind of negative behavior, creating the conditions for extended and recurring acts of violence.

In the world of business, norms of reciprocity may also lead to negative repercussions if the norms push individuals to engage in behaviors that undermine the common good. When corruption sets in, organizations may reinforce behaviors that support illegal activities, as we have noted. The infamous case of Enron provides evidence that organizational norms can be effective in hiding corruption and bolstering support for illegal activities, especially when those involved stand to gain from these activities. Monitoring and sanctioning mechanisms are typically put in place in these situations to make sure those involved are abiding by the norms that foster network closure and the capacity to keep such activities from the light of day. In such situations, laws that protect whistleblowers are needed, in addition to regulatory frameworks that are effective. In the end it is hard to maintain the secrecy needed to cover up the illegal activities involved once they become common knowledge. A more recent example is the case of Theranos in California in which a faulty blood test was touted to investors as having broad-ranging capacities to detect a variety of health conditions, a claim that was not accurate and in fact misleading. That case is now in court and witnesses are coming forward to tell the story of how critical facts were hidden from the view of investors as well as many company employees. Internal organizational norms and practices regarding who had access to information were implicated in efforts to hide relevant facts as the product (the testing machine) was being developed and produced (Carreyrou 2018).

3.6   Concluding comments

Norms have long been the object of study in the social sciences, and they have varied in significance in efforts to explain human behavior and social organization. In sociology they often take center stage in such endeavors. Talcott Parsons, whose work was influential for many years beginning in the 1930s until roughly around the 1970s, was a key proponent of the major influence of social norms and values in society. These terms were among the primary concepts in his theories of social action and his approach to the analysis of social behavior as socially constrained both by existing norms and by prevalent social structures. What followed was a debate that has persisted over the years concerning the prominence of this "oversocialized" view of humans (cf., Wrong 1961) whose behavior is controlled by the very existence of norms. Failure to abide by them is conceptualized simply as deviance. As Wrong notes, this oversimplifies the problem of social order and treats humans as having less agency in the long run. In contrast, the more rational choice conceptions of action have been criticized for treating humans as "undersocialized," as driven more by self-interest and less with concerns about others. This debate continues.

In spite of a lack of resolution to this debate, there has been a revival of interest during the past few decades, even among economists, in the role of norms and values, not just in terms of social behavior and change but also in the realm of political behavior and economic activity. What Coleman (1987b) points out is that we do not yet have a clear idea of what combination of internalization and external sanctions is efficient, a kind of middle ground between more sociological conceptions of action and the dominant economic approaches. This judgment remains accurate today.

Putnam (1995, 2000, etc.) directed attention to the role of norms in furthering collective action and civic participation, a role he viewed as central to the study of social capital and its effects in society. Without strong norms of reciprocity, fostered by social connection, Putnam viewed the United States as moving toward a cliff at the dawn of the twenty-first century, on the verge of falling into a state of disillusionment with our once hallowed halls of democracy. This prognosis was fairly accurate, even though no one could actually have clearly foreseen the full impact of the events of the 2010s and 2020s. And, other countries have faced similar challenges, not just politically, but also in terms of social unrest, as well as health and environmental issues posed by pandemics and climate change. It was not just weakening norms of reciprocity that concerned Putnam. He included this aspect as part of the mix of social capital factors "at fault" in the decline of civil society and its downstream effects. As we have noted, however, unless we tease apart these separate dimensions of social capital it is hard to fully understand the mechanisms involved in the social changes he forecasted and even more difficult to make policy prescriptions to mitigate the most negative consequences of the "loss of social capital." We discuss this issue further in Chapter 5.

Norms of all kinds are important in understanding human behavior. Our quick take on them is that they emerge out of behavioral regularities that become taken for granted, and they can change over time as new behaviors and strategies for social action take hold. Once they do take hold, by whatever mechanism that happens, they become part of the fabric of social life and serve as guides for "expected behavior." They can be either purely descriptive or they can carry moral force, but they clearly play a role in everyday behavior in all contexts, large and small. The focus of our discussion, led by Putnam's emphasis, is on norms of reciprocity without which we can't easily imagine daily life. It is a kind of "tit for tat" notion and under some circumstances encourages us to "pay it forward" as we move to more generalized reciprocity (or generalized exchange based on it). In this sense it is important in understanding human coop-eration and the maintenance of general social order.

Without guard rails on acceptable behavior, it is not clear how social order can be maintained (unless by the use of force), as we see during periods of social and political malaise and major conflicts. What we have yet to fully determine is how norms emerge and become taken for granted. And even though it appears that reciprocity is somewhat "hard-wired," we can't typically just rely on reciprocity norms, in part because we often draw boundaries around those to which the norm applies. Does it apply to family, friends, and co-workers only? When does the norm apply to those considered "outsiders" or strangers? Are such norms central to maintaining social connection and social order and do they undergird the emergence of trust? We address some of these issues in the next chapter on trust.

Notes

1. "According to Coleman, social capital can take on three forms; (1) obliga-tions and expectations which depend on the trustworthiness of the social environment, (2) the capacity of information to flow through the social structure in order to provide a basis for action and (3) *the presence of norms accompanied by effective sanctions*" (Report of the Office of National Statistics 2001, emphasis added).
2. The importance of strong leaders in communities for building on existing social capital to resolve collective action problems and foster economic development is also noted by Krishna (2002) in a study of 69 villages in North India.

References

Agrawal, Arun (1999). *Greener Pastures: Politics, Markets, and Community among a Migrant Pastoral People*. Durham, NC: Duke University Press.

Blau, Peter M. (2002). "Reflections on a Career as a Theorist." Pp. 345–57 in Joseph Berger and Morris Zelditch Jr. (eds.), *New Directions in Contemporary Sociological Theory*. Lanham, MD: Rowman & Littlefield.

Braithwaite, John (1998). "Institutionalizing Distrust, Enculturating Trust." Pp. 343–75 in Valerie Braithwaite and Margaret Levi (eds.), *Trust & Governance*. New York: Russell Sage Foundation.

Carreyrou, John (2018). *Bad Blood: Secrets and Lies in a Silicon Valley Startup*. New York: Alfred A. Knopf.

Cialdini, Robert B. (1996). "The Triple Tumor Structure of Organizational Behavior." Pp. 44–58 in David M. Messick and Anne E. Tenbrunsel (eds.), *Codes of Conduct: Behavioral Research into Business Ethics*. New York: Russell Sage Foundation.

Cohen, Jean (1999). "Trust, Voluntary Association and Workable Democracy: The Contemporary American Discourse of Civil Society." Pp. 108–248 in Mark E. Warren (ed.), *Democracy & Trust*. Cambridge: Cambridge University Press.

Cohen, Marc A. and Mathew S. Isaac (2021). "Trust Does Beget Trustworthiness and Also Begets Trust in Others." *Social Psychology Quarterly* 84(2): 189–201.

Coleman, James S. (1987a). "Externalities and Norms in a Linear System of Action." Working Paper, Department of Sociology, University of Chicago.

Coleman, James S. (1987b). "Norms as Social Capital." Pp. 133–55 in G. Radnitzky and P. Bernholz (eds.), *Economic Imperialism: The Economic Approach Applied Outside the Field of Economics*. New York: Paragon House.

Coleman, James S. (1988). "Social Capital in the Creation of Human Capital." *American Journal of Sociology* 94: S95–S121.

Cook, Karen S. (2005). "Networks, Norms and Trust: The Social Psychology of Social Capital." *Social Psychology Quarterly* 68(1): 4–14.

Cook, Karen S. and Robin M. Cooper (2003). "Experimental Studies of Cooperation, Trust and Social Exchange." Pp. 209–44 in Elinor Ostrom and James Walker (eds.), *Trust & Reciprocity: Interdisciplinary Lessons from Experimental Research*. New York: Russell Sage Foundation.

Cook, Karen S. and Russell Hardin (2001). "Norms of Cooperativeness and Networks of Trust." Pp. 327–47 in Michael Hechter and Karl Dieter Opp (eds.), *Social Norms*. New York: Russell Sage Foundation.

Cook, Karen S., Russell Hardin, and Margaret Levi (2005). *Cooperation without Trust?* New York: Russell Sage Foundation.

de Waal, Frans B.M. (1989). "Food Sharing and Reciprocal Obligations Among Chimpanzees." *Journal of Human Evolution* 18: 433–59.

de Waal, Frans B.M. (2000). "Attitudinal Reciprocity in Food Sharing Among Brown Capuchins." *Animal Behaviour* 60: 253–61.

de Waal, Frans B.M. (2003). "The Chimpanzee's Service Economy: Evidence for Cognition-Based Reciprocal Exchange." Pp. 128–43 in Elinor Ostrom and James Walker (eds.), *Trust & Reciprocity: Interdisciplinary Lessons from Experimental Research*. New York: Russell Sage Foundation.

Durkheim, Emile ([1895] 1982). *Rules of the Sociological Method*. New York: Free Press.

Ellickson, Robert C. (2001). "The Evolution of Social Norms: A Perspective from the Legal Academy." Pp. 35–75 in Michael Hechter and Karl-Dieter Opp (eds.), *Social Norms*. New York: Russell Sage Foundation.

Fehr, Ernst and Simon Gaechter (2000). "Fairness and Retaliation: The Economics of Reciprocity." *Journal of Economic Perspectives* 14: 159–81.

Fischer, Claude (1982). *To Dwell Among Friends: Personal Networks in Town and City*. Chicago, IL: University of Chicago Press.

Frey, Bruno (1994). "How Intrinsic Motivation is Crowded In and Out." *Rationality and Society* 6: 334–52.

Gambetta, Diego (1993). *The Sicilian Mafia*. London: Harvard University Press.

Gouldner, A. (1960). "The Norm of Reciprocity: A Preliminary Statement." *American Sociological Review* 25: 161–78.

Graeff, Peter (2009). "Social Capital: The Dark Side." Pp. 143–61 in Gert Tinggaard Svendsen and Gunnar Lind Haase Svendsen (eds.), *Handbook of Social Capital: The Troika of Sociology, Political Science and Economics*. Cheltenham, UK and Northampton, MA, USA: Edward Elgar Publishing.

Halpern, David (2005). *Social Capital*. Cambridge: Polity Press.

Hechter, Michael and Karl-Dieter Opp (2001). "What Have We Learned about the Emergence of Norms?" Pp. 394–415 in Michael Hechter and Karl-Dieter Opp (eds.), *Social Norms*. New York: Russell Sage Foundation.

Irwin, Kyle and Brent Simpson (2013). "Do Descriptive Norms Solve Social Dilemmas? Conformity and Contributions in Collective Action Groups." *Social Forces* 91(3): 1057–84.

Krishna, Anirudh (2002). *Active Social Capital: Tracing the Roots of Development and Democracy*. New York: Columbia University Press.

Lawler, Edward J., Shane R. Thye, and Jeongkoo Yoon (2008). "Social Exchange and Micro Social Order." *American Sociological Review* 73(4): 519–42.

Malhotra, D. and J.K. Murnighan (2002). "The Effects of Contracts on Interpersonal Trust." *Administrative Science Quarterly* 47: 534–59.

McCabe, Kevin A. (2003). "A Cognitive Theory of Reciprocal Exchange." Pp. 147–69 in Elinor Ostrom and James Walker (eds.), *Trust & Reciprocity: Interdisciplinary Lessons from Experimental Research*. New York: Russell Sage Foundation.

McKean, M.A. (1986). "Management of Traditional Common Lands (Iriaichi) in Japan." Pp. 533–89 in *Proceedings of the Conference on Common Resource Property Management*. National Research Council. Washington, DC: National Academy Press.

Molm, Linda D. (1997). *Coercive Power in Social Exchange*. Cambridge: Cambridge University Press.

Molm, Linda D. (2010). "The Structure of Reciprocity." *Social Psychology Quarterly* 73(2): 119–31.

Mulder, L.B., E. Van Dijk, D. De Cremer, and H.A.M. Wilke (2006). "Undermining Trust and Cooperation: The Paradox of Sanctioning Systems in Social Dilemmas." *Journal of Experimental Social Psychology* 42: 147–62.

Olson, Mancur (1965). *The Logic of Collective Action: Public Goods and the Theory of Groups*. Cambridge, MA: Harvard University Press.

Ostrom, Elinor (1990). *Governing the Commons: The Evolution of Institutions for Collective Action*. New York: Cambridge University Press.

Ostrom, Elinor (2000). "Collective Action and the Evolution of Social Norms." *Journal of Economic Perspectives* 14(3): 137–58.

Ostrom, Elinor (2003). "Toward a Behavioral Theory Linking Trust, Reciprocity, and Reputation." Pp. 19–79 in Elinor Ostrom and James Walker (eds.), *Trust & Reciprocity: Interdisciplinary Lessons from Experimental Research*. New York: Russell Sage Foundation.

Posner, Eric (2000). *Law and Social Norms*. Cambridge, MA: Harvard University Press.

Putnam, Robert D. (1995). "Bowling Alone: American's Declining Social Capital." *Journal of Democracy* 6: 65–78.

Putnam, Robert D. (2000). *Bowling Alone: The Collapse and Revival of American Community*. New York: Simon & Schuster.

Putnam, Robert D. (2020). *The Upswing: How America Came Together a Century Ago and How We Can Do It Again*. New York: Simon & Schuster.

Simpson, Brent and Robb Willer (2015). "Beyond Altruism: Sociological Foundations of Cooperation and Prosocial Behavior." *Annual Review of Sociology* 41: 43–61.

Simpson, Brent, Robb Willer, and Ashley Harrell (2017). "Reinforcement of Moral Boundaries Promotes Cooperation and Prosocial Behavior in Groups." *Scientific Reports* 7(1): http://doi.org/10.1038/srep42844.

Simpson, Brent, Ashley Harrell, David Melamed, Nicholas Heiserman, and Daniela V. Negraia (2018). "The Roots of Reciprocity: Gratitude and Reputation in Generalized Exchange Systems." *American Sociological Review* 83(1): 88–110.

Sutter, M., S. Haigner, and M.G. Kocher (2010). "Choosing the Carrot or the Stick? Endogenous Institutional Choice in Social Dilemma Situations." *Review of Economic Studies* 77: 1540–66.

Uslaner, Eric M. (2009). "Corruption." Pp. 127–42 in Gert Tinggaard Svendsen and Gunnar Lind Haase Svendsen (eds.), *Handbook of Social Capital: The*

Troika of Sociology, Political Science and Economics. Cheltenham, UK and Northampton, MA, USA: Edward Elgar Publishing.

Varese, Frederico (2004). "Mafia Transplantation." Pp. 148–66 in Janos Kornai, Bo Rothstein, and Susan Rose-Ackerman (eds.), *Creating Social Trust in Post-Socialist Transition.* New York: Palgrave Macmillan.

Whitman, Monica M. (2021). "Generalized Generosities: How the Norm of Generalized Reciprocity Bridges Collective Forms of Exchange." *American Sociological Review* 86(3): 503–31.

Wrong, Dennis (1961). "The Oversocialized Conception of Man in Modern Sociology." *American Sociological Review* 26(2): 183–93.

4   Trust

... in the early 1960s nearly two thirds of Americans trusted other people, but two decades into the twenty-first century two thirds of Americans did not.
(Putnam 2020: 159)

Trust is often argued to be key to facilitating cooperation and social order in society. To the extent that trust exists in others in society and in the significant organizations and institutions in which one's life is embedded, cooperation is easier, and the costs of monitoring and sanctioning are reduced, if not eliminated. For Coleman (1988), as well as Putnam (Putnam, Leonardi, and Nanetti 1993; Putnam 2000), it is for this reason that trust is considered a form of social capital when it exists in a social organization or between individuals in a network, group, or community. But we gain no particular analytical purchase by referring to trust as social capital. So, we will simply treat it separately as a fact of social life or social organization that yields various benefits when it is warranted. Trust, when not warranted, may lead to exploitation or other negative outcomes, including corruption and physical harm. So, trust cannot be viewed as a universal good. As Newton (2007: 345) writes: "In modern, large-scale, geographically mobile, mixed and multicultural societies, trust in strangers is particularly important, especially in strangers who are not like us." Generalized trust is key to the social integration and stability of modern society, Newton goes on to argue. In this chapter we discuss the role that this generalized social trust has in society and in the networks that connect people and provide social capital or access to resources of value. We also note its limitations and clarify the different roles that generalized trust and particularized trust play at the community and societal levels.

We begin with Putnam's claims about the role of general societal trust as a form of social capital. However, we discuss trust and its effects without labeling it "social capital" to gain conceptual clarity. As Stolle (2007: 660) notes,

> Putnam's work builds on Almond and Verba ... who argued that a culture of trust is one of the important prerequisites to democratic stability. Here trust refers not only to general social trust in others, but also to confidence in important societal institutions. Inglehart ... claims that economic development leads to certain cultural changes, particularly in trust, which help to stabilize democracy. In his view, a culture of trust serves as an essential underpinning to the acceptance of democratic rules, for example, allowing the opposition to take over after an election.

This comment, made two decades before the 2020 elections in the United States, was prescient. I do not think anyone could have predicted the occurrence of a challenge to the duly elected president by the outgoing president, let alone the riotous mob that stormed the U.S. Capitol and caused the loss of life, serious wounds to many, and extensive property damage, all in the name of a "stolen election," a false claim made by Donald J. Trump in the Fall of 2020. He lost the valid election by over five million votes. His numerous court cases challenging vote tallies in various states were all declared baseless in law. In states where recounts were conducted, the original results in every case were confirmed. It had definitely been a "free and fair" election by all accounts.

Two factors were most relevant. First, few predicted that a president, when confronted with the facts concerning the outcome of an election, would fail to acknowledge that he had lost and engage in actions that inspired his supporters to riot in order to stop the confirmation of the results in congressional action to validate the Electoral College outcome. Al Gore, who lost to George Bush by a very slim margin, had not done so. Second, it is precisely the breakdown in "the culture of trust that supports the acceptance of democratic rules" (Stolle 2007: 660) and institutions that fueled such extreme reactions to the election (in addition to the incitement to react by the outgoing president). Trust in government was at an all-time low in the U.S.A. when these events took place. In many countries, the confidence or trust of citizens that their government will "do the right thing" is at the heart of their willingness to engage in civic activity and follow the dictates of governmental entities.

Given the importance of general trust in the institutions at the core of any society we begin this chapter with a commentary on trust in government.

As Letki (2018: 339) argues, "People who trust others and those who have confidence in political institutions are more likely to pay taxes, vote, follow politics, and join political parties, and voluntary associations" (see also Howard 2003; Uslaner 2003; Letki 2004, 2006). This quote reveals why Putnam viewed this form of social capital as important in supporting not only political activities and democratic institutions, but also in facilitating collective action for the public good undergirding civil society and fostering social order.

4.1   Trust in government

Clearly, the riots in the Capitol were a stark reminder of the extent to which citizen trust in the United States government had declined. Even when Putnam (2000) was writing about declines in social capital, one of his key indicators was the rapid drop in trust in government. Putnam notes that in the mid-1960s, citizens were more confident in general in their political institutions and government representatives. At that time "Three in four said that you could 'trust the government in Washington to do what is right all or most of the time'" (Putnam 2000: 47). In this same passage he goes on to indicate that by the 1990s it had reversed: by then "roughly three in four Americans didn't trust the government to do what is right most of the time." The level of trust in government at the time of the riots in the U.S. Capitol, two decades later, had fallen to an all-time low, particularly among those who participated, following a president unwilling to accept his electoral fate, fueling active distrust. What we know from the Pew surveys is that, for varying reasons, in 2020 only about 20 percent of Americans trusted the government to "do the right thing" (Figure 4.1).

Over the decades, many political theorists have written about trust in government at the federal, state, and local levels and some of them view trust (or confidence) as essential to the smooth functioning of government, especially for democratic regimes. Governments often resort to more autocratic or coercive means of ruling when they do not enjoy the consent and compliance of those they govern. Levi (1988, 1997), among others, has argued that the basis for compliance is belief in governmental effectiveness and the perceived procedural fairness of those who govern and the institutions in which they are embedded. These factors undergird

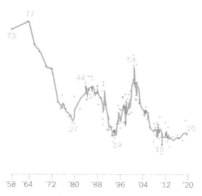

Source: Pew Research Center (2019).

Figure 4.1   Trust in government over six decades

citizen trust. The examples she provides are of citizens' tax compliance and their willingness to submit to conscription, two behaviors that tend to be based on confidence in and the perceived legitimacy of government.

The putative basis for trust in government, however, varies among theorists. In Putnam's work, trust among citizens leads to more civic engagement and a stronger civil society. These are the factors he identifies as having a stabilizing effect in society, increasing social order and the governability of citizens. In such argumentation it is trust of the citizens of each other that provides the foundation for a more cooperative and productive society as well as more effective governance. For these political theorists, trust within the citizenry matters and it has a spillover effect on the capacity for good governance and the related trust in governmental institutions. But we are left wondering what is the basis for trust among the citizens and how does it emerge?

Other political theorists place stock in trust in institutions as creating the grounds for trust within the citizenry or more generalized trust in the society. These theorists (e.g., Levi 1997; Levi and Stoker 2000) view trust in the institutions of governance as the glue that binds society together and fosters social order. Good government provides support for strong institutions that enforce laws and give citizens the assurance they need that when trust fails, they have recourse. Keele (2007) focuses on the role of government performance, as do Levi (1997) and Tarrow (1996) in understanding the conditions required to produce trust or confidence in the institutions of government supporting the emergence of trust among citizens. These conditions include effectiveness and procedural fairness.

Another key factor in predicting trust in government is the extent of inequality in society (particularly socio-economic inequality). As evidenced by the Nordic countries and other modern welfare states, less inequality within society and low levels of corruption often foster higher levels of trust in government as well as generalized trust among citizens. For example, in Denmark, Sweden, and Norway, over 60 percent of those surveyed in the World Values Survey (WVS) (Wave IV, 1999–2000) indicated that "most people can be trusted," the highest percentages across the countries included in the study (Newton 2007: 347). In this same article, Newton also includes data from the same WVS indicating that 50 percent or more of those surveyed in Denmark, Norway, and Sweden responded that they had "a great deal or quite a lot" of confidence in parliament. Countries near the bottom of this scale include some in the former Soviet Union (e.g., Ukraine, Estonia, Bulgaria, Lithuania) and some in Latin America (e.g., Argentina, Peru, Brazil). These are countries with a past or current history of authoritarian rule and often high levels of inequality.

With respect to authoritarian rule, Halpern (2005: 269), among others, suggests that "the preponderance of rigid and strongly hierarchical social structures" is characteristic of low social capital societies, particularly those with low social trust among the citizens. Power differences are sharp and reduce the capacity for wide-ranging social trust. In addition, Halpern (2005) posits that too little attention has been paid to economic inequality in the early work on social capital, which seems to paint too rosy a picture of the positive effects of social capital in society, a sweeping claim. In an analysis of the causes of differential levels of social capital across nations Halpern (2005: 271) writes that "inequality stretches the social fabric, increasing social distance between individuals and reducing the likelihood of shared interests, social associations, norms of mutual respect," thus impacting levels of social trust as well. We delve more deeply into the role of inequality later in this chapter.

An interesting caveat in the literature on trust in government is that local government officials are often viewed as more trustworthy than those in the federal government (Pew Research Center 2019). Some argue that this is due to the fact that citizens often have more information at the local level on which to base assessments of trustworthiness. The actions of local government officials typically have more immediate and visible effects.

4.2   Trust in other institutions

In addition to trust in the institutions associated with governing a society, there are other key societal institutions. These include those that promote religion, develop scientific knowledge, and provide medical break-throughs as well as treatments for diseases and other health-related conditions. In fact, some of these institutions have also seen a decline in trust not only in the United States, but also in other places around the globe. With the exception of confidence or trust in the scientific community, which has remained relatively stable over time, trust in medicine, organized religion, and education has declined over time (Smith and Son, 2013).[1] More recent evidence is consistent with these trends, though they are somewhat complicated by the global pandemic and the unique circumstances surrounding the Trump presidency in the U.S.A. In fact, trust in science and medicine was shaken for many during the four years of this administration, associated most directly with the (mis)management of the coronavirus pandemic. As noted above, confidence in the institutions of government, especially Congress, was the lowest it had been since the General Survey was first conducted in the early 1970s (see also Figure 4.3). At the same time, the military seems to be immune to the vicissitudes of politics as confidence in military leaders increased while trust in other institutions declined (Figures 4.2 and 4.3 include recent data).

Trust in organized religion, specifically religious leaders, took a major hit when revelations of abuse by clergy members surfaced in the United States, as in many other countries. In addition, business leaders, journalists, and elected officials were viewed as less trustworthy (even more so than religious leaders) by members of the public in 2020. Note that these data were collected by Pew about a month after the pandemic shutdown across many parts of the country. They also indicate that trust in science, and medical science more specifically, remained fairly high (despite challenging conditions) and this factor may have contributed to the speed at which vaccines were able to be produced and later circulated throughout the population, even though there were certainly strong pockets of recalcitrance often based on political ideology and, to some extent, unfounded

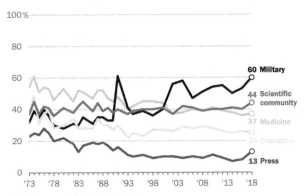

Source: Pew Research Center (2019).

Figure 4.2   General Social Survey (GSS) data on confidence in some institutions in the U.S.A. 1973–2018

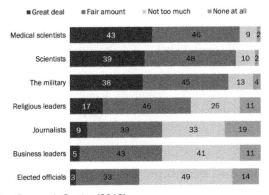

Source: Pew Research Center (2019).

Figure 4.3   Data on trust in selected institutions 2019

fears of side-effects or concerns over the rushed nature of the vaccine development leading to emergency authorization by the Federal Drug Administration (FDA). Even after full authorization of the vaccines by the FDA there remained a fairly large contingent of committed anti-vaccine proponents.

Trust or confidence in societal institutions, whether focused on governing or on other aspects of life including the exercise of religion, business activity, and educational pursuits, makes a difference in the lives of citizens and their decisions concerning engagement with these institutions. For instance, when trust in organized religion and the leaders of various sects declined, so too did church attendance and religious contributions. Lower levels of trust in the educational system often leads to the formation of alternative schools, outside the realm of public education and its regulations. Lower levels of trust in the media and various press outlets, including those who produce content, reduces the knowledge level of the citizenry, with deleterious consequences leading to actions that may even circumvent the law, given that they are based on false information or what are often called "alternative facts" such as the "Big Lie" concerning the outcome of the 2020 elections in the U.S.A., a view that continues to reverberate in American politics. Even the right to vote is up for grabs.

Trust in institutions and those who lead them also affects the level of general social trust in others, especially in strangers. This fact relates to evidence that general social trust is higher in societies in which there is democratic rule and confidence in the legal institutions that provide the basis for engagement in various forms with those one does not know – in contracting with them, completing transactions with them, joining them in social activities, and even entering certain kinds of relationships with them that may endure. In addition, when institutional trust facilitates social trust, it also facilitates economic activities, as many economists have documented in the literature on social capital.

4.3   Trust and economic development

There is an influential and somewhat contentious stream of research on the nature of the connections of various forms of social capital to economic development. The main focus of Fukuyama's (1995) widely read book on social trust, for example, was the nature of its link to national prosperity in a number of countries. While some of the early work on social capital, building on Putnam's main thesis, investigated the role of civic engagement in the political realm and involvement with local civic associations in economic development, subsequent work directed attention primarily to the role of generalized trust. The main reason was that, following Fukuyama's lead, general social trust had a much stronger empirical association with various measures of economic development than did the existing measures of civic engagement. In addition, there were more generally available measures of social trust in surveys across a number of countries in the world, making it easier to examine its connection with existing indicators of economic growth over time. As Fukuyama (1995: 27) notes: "Widespread distrust in a society ... imposes a kind of tax on all forms of economic activity, a tax that high-trust societies do not have to pay." This tax includes the costs of monitoring, enforcement, and developing general regulations to deter corruption and secure transactions. Besides well-functioning and reliable institutions, generalized trust within the citizenry lowers such transaction costs, as Arrow (1974) argued in the early 1970s. What continues to be debated in economics is the causal role of general social trust and the other dimensions of social capital. Some economists argue that there are more direct causal factors relating to production, innovation, and corruption that are salient in the path to economic development.

Fukuyama's (1995) book on social trust, which attracted the attention of politicians and business leaders, compares countries in which much of the economic activity is based on familial networks in contrast with those in which it is based on relations characterized by generalized trust. And, in his view, it is this transition from tighter kin-based networks to open networks of exchange that facilitates the move to markets and the growth of the economy, as we have discussed in Chapter 2. To simplify, he argues that familial trust, based on long-term, thick relationships, supports the development of small-scale enterprises much like those created in ethnic enclaves of immigrants in the American context. But these same factors do not support economic activities that extend beyond the confines of those tightly knit boundaries. Engagement with "outsiders" or strangers in economic and social exchange at least initially requires some basis for more generalized trust, some reason for taking the risk (especially in the context of weak institutions). And there is some evidence that strong family-based trust is negatively correlated with trust in strangers, that is, it lowers general trust (Ermisch and Gambetta 2010).

Bjornskov (2018) reviews the research on linkages between general trust and economic growth, commenting on various direct and indirect mechanisms that have been argued to underlie these effects. In his view, trust "greases the wheels of innovation" and the related economic production that fuels growth. Indirectly social norms that prohibit exploitation and "self-dealing" are identified as important in societies in which general social trust is high and such norms lead people to engage in self-restraint. In part, people are concerned with maintaining reputations for trustworthiness that are especially important in societies in which many network-based transactions occur and one's reputation is the coin of the realm in terms of long-term economic success. General trust may also have direct effects on economic productivity and growth (Zak and Knack 2001) through increases in investments more broadly, given that transactions are secured and institutions provide assurance (when they do).

However, some data suggest that generalized trust (treated by Putnam as an indicator of social capital) is not the key causal factor in predicting the "grand transition" between being a relatively poor country with low trust and a wealthier country with high trust, as suggested in Putnam's claim of the centrality of social capital to economic development (see Paldam 2009). A number of other factors are involved, including those related to the nature of the state and its role in improving (or not) the welfare of its citizens, as well as larger legal, global, and environmental variables. Although generalized trust is indicated as an important driver of production linked to economic development, due mainly to its role in reducing the need for monitoring and sanctioning, decreasing transaction costs result. It may not be the most salient determinant. Most important for the economy is confidence in the relevant institutions.

With respect to trust, the correlations between income and generalized trust are significant, reflecting the importance of income and welfare in the level of generalized trust in a society. Paldam's (2009: 355) findings based on the WVS from 1980 to 2000 on income and generalized trust replicate the cultural clustering of countries by trust levels found in other studies. The best-known example, as we have noted, is the Nordic countries that have the highest levels of generalized trust in the world, and low levels of inequality. In fact, in a study of economic growth in 29 countries, Knack and Keefer (1997) found more generally that relatively equal incomes and higher levels of ethnic homogeneity (as exists in the Nordic countries) are associated with higher levels of trust and stronger civic norms. In contrast, countries with higher levels of inequality and low levels of social trust are, unfortunately, more susceptible to corruption.

4.4   The lack of trust and corruption

In addition to low social trust (in one another), low levels of institutional trust are associated with an increase in corruption in society. One reason is that weak institutions that do not engender the trust of those they serve are breeding grounds for illegal activity and efforts to bribe or otherwise reward those who would circumvent existing norms and rules to provide services of value. In some societies, "bribes" are even "required" to obtain services, even those that are available from government, not private sources. In Hungary, for example, Kornai (1996) documents the existence of "side payments" used to obtain higher-quality medical services during and after the post-socialist transition. According to Letki (2018), such actions have negative consequences, specifically in transition economies. "Unofficial payments in order to secure access to key goods and services reduce citizens' confidence in institutions' transparency and efficiency" (Letki 2018: 346), further weakening support for institutional reform in these "grey economies."

The level of corruption, especially in government institutions, influences individuals' assessments not only of the system in which those institutions are embedded, but also of their fellow citizens. Distrust of the system breeds distrust among citizens (Montinola 2004). Opportunities for corrupt transactions or side payments are sometimes limited by transparency, but not always. In many government institutions, bureaucrats may act in their own self-interest or the interest of their family members and close associates rather than in the interest of the institution, particularly when such behavior is not likely to be detected or sanctioned, if discovered. Tolerance of this type of corrupt behavior when it violates organizational rules and norms creates a slippery slope in which others engage in similar behaviors and corruption increases, thus feeding the vicious cycle.

As Montinola argues (2004: 305): "Even if there appear to be certain regularities in corrupt regimes, such as an implicit understanding regarding the size of bribes, the illegal and clandestine nature of the corrupt transactions inhibits the emergence of trust." When governments commit to implementing policies in nonarbitrary fashion, following rules of procedural justice and fairness, they create the basis not only for trust in government (Levi 1998), but also for trust among the citizens because they understand that there is accountability and the appropriate enforcement of fair treatment. In Montinola's (2004) case study, she finds that the justices in the Philippine Supreme Court (which was restructured to counter a strong executive branch by a constitution in 1987) increasingly engaged in corrupt behavior as a result of increased incentives and opportunity, in the face of weakened accountability.

Montinola (2004: 316) concludes that "The perception of widespread corruption … is sufficient to provide grounds to distrust government, to distrust fellow citizens, and to continue to depend on corrupt means to ensure one's well-being." Her work provides evidence of a cycle of corruption and distrust that in the end is self-defeating in institutions and societies in which it is set in motion. When it occurs in the context of widespread inequality this cycle has come to be known as the "inequality trap" (Uslaner 2008b) and we find it in many countries around the world. In Uslaner's (2009) model, inequality and corruption are linked indirectly through trust. Inequality leads to low levels of generalized trust and high in-group (or particularized) trust, which leads to corruption. And corruption breeds inequality by "turning people inward and reducing the sanctions … for taking advantage of others" (Uslaner 2009: 135), hence the trap, which Uslaner finds strong support for across the 61 nations included in his study.

In countries in which trust in institutions is low due to corruption, and the lack of transparency and interpersonal business transactions are rife with dishonesty and contract infringement, informal social relations develop over time as a way of securing transactions. Reputations play a large role as partners share stories of cheating and dishonesty to reduce contract failure and to eliminate bad actors. Radaev (2004) writes about his interviews with business associates in Russia just after the transition period, post-socialism. Those involved in business develop reputations as honest dealers or defectors – rule breakers. The defectors, Radaev (2004: 104) notes, are "stigmatized as otmorozki (following no rules) and chermushniki (black dealers) whose actions are damaging for the market." What develops is a form of mutual trust built primarily on closed networks, repeat interactions, and predictability, only sometimes produced by state policies supporting formal and informal rules. Unlike other societies in which kin relations help to secure transactions, in Russia even these "affect-based" trust relations were not predictable; thus, they moved to a focus on reputations that could extend the circle of business associates. In these closed networks, good reputations were the coin of the realm. In Russia, the distrust of institutions runs deep.

In additional studies of the link between social trust and corruption in different forms of government, some researchers interestingly report a stronger effect of corruption on trust in government and in people in some democratic regimes. This is the case in part because there may be greater opportunity in both the private sector and the public welfare sector for opportunistic behavior that is viewed as undermining confidence, especially if impartiality and lack of fairness are characteristic of the delivery of widespread welfare and other social services. The impact of such behavior in autocratic societies may be more limited because corruption may be concentrated among those in power (see You 2018). You (2015) argues that "it is inequality that fuels corruption in democracies by increasing clientelism, patronage and elite capture" (cited in You 2018: 492). While it is clear that there is a link between social trust and corruption, the actual causal direction remains somewhat unclear. The association may lead either to virtuous or vicious cycles, depending on level and the effectiveness of legal remedies.

There is some evidence associating trust and corruption in earlier research, following Putnam's finding that in Italy regions with lower social trust had higher levels of political corruption. And You (2018: 481) cites others including La Porta, Lopez-de-Salinas, Shleifer, and Vishny (1997) who "find strong cross-national evidence of the beneficial effect of social trust on corruption control." Uslaner (2008a) provides an analysis of survey data from Romania and Estonia suggesting that "particularized trust facilitates corruption, whereas generalized trust deters corruption" (cited in You 2018: 482). This finding supports the argument made in Chapter 2 that closed networks in which mutual trust exists can be a breeding ground for illegal activity, such as the criminal activities of Mafia-type organizations, or such networks can be an important source of virtuous activity such as the provision of the kinds of public goods that we discuss next. The questions we address specifically are how and when does social trust facilitate collective action?

4.5   Trust and collective action

Social trust, and the resulting collective orientation it often produces, may increase civic engagement in neighborhoods and communities, as well as commitment to actions that provide public goods, one of

Putnam's (Putnam, Leonardi, and Nanetti 1993; Putnam 2007) claims about the significance of social capital. The provision of a public good fits the definition of what is called a social dilemma in the social science literature. A straightforward definition is offered by Van Lange, Balliet, Parks, and Van Vugt (2014: 11) in their review of interdisciplinary work on this topic. They define "social dilemmas as situations in which a non-cooperative course of action is (at times) tempting for individuals in that it yields superior outcomes (often short-term) for self, and if all pursue this non-cooperative course of action, all are (often in the longer-term) worse off than if all had cooperated." In a simple two-person context this situation is referred to as the "prisoner's dilemma," referring to the conundrum faced by those who are guilty deciding whether to confess or not with clear implications for the outcomes of both parties (e.g., to go free or to jail).

Some of the most important work on the role of trust in collective actions entailing such social dilemmas has been conducted by Elinor Ostrom and her collaborators. In a handbook article on social capital and collective action, Ostrom and Ahn (2009) treat social capital as a "rubric" having three components: (1) trustworthiness, (2) networks, and (3) formal and informal rules or institutions (a version of Putnam's definition). They view "social capital as an attribute of individuals and of their relationships that enhance their ability to solve collective action problems" (Ostrom and Ahn 2009: 20). To get more explicit they develop a model that explains collective action, indicating specifically how these three components of social capital are linked through trust, the factor they define as central to the solution of collective action problems (Figure 4.4).

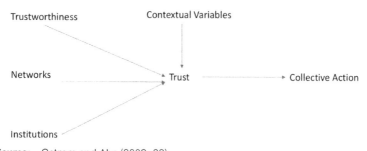

Source: Ostrom and Ahn (2009: 23).

Figure 4.4   Model of the role of trust in collective action

Trust is produced, Ostrom and Ahn (2009: 22) argue, when "individuals are trustworthy, are networked with one another and are in institutions that reward honest behavior." It is thus the trustworthiness of people, networks, and institutions that explains the existence of the trust that facilitates collective action in many contexts. The networks and institutions in which individuals are embedded enhance trust by changing the incentives involved to be trustworthy. Others in their networks can view their behavior over time and sanction bad actors. Reputations circulate within networks to constrain such "bad behavior." Given that reputations have significant value in groups, communities, and even small networks, individuals invest in maintaining a reputation for being trustworthy and for sanctioning those who are not. For Ostrom (2003), this fact supports evolutionary thinking indicating that building reputations for keeping promises increases "fitness" in situations in which others base their behavior on reciprocity norms.

The relevant institutions, through rules and laws, provide the rewards or punishments that are to be assessed. Institutions are viewed quite broadly as composed of rules and/or laws of behavior. They can be formal or informal and they are key to producing the trust and subsequent cooperation required for collective action of all types, either for the common good or for darker purposes. Gambetta's (1988) research on the Mafia is a good example of the latter, as we have indicated. Closed trust networks built on family bonds and ties to close associates within the Mafia allow for tight control, effective monitoring, and often swift (and sometimes harsh) sanctions. Strong within-group trust in this case leads to actions that foster the needs and nefarious activities of the Mafia, even if they undermine broader community goals and social cohesion (see also Chapters 2 and 3). In such settings, as Portes (1998: 6) argues, trust exists "because obligations are enforceable, not through recourse to law or violence but through the power of community."

Related work on the role of trust in social dilemmas more generally helps us identify other key factors that facilitate or hinder the development of solutions to collective action problems. Some are located at the individual level, others at the community level, as Ostrom's work makes clear. At the individual level, research clearly indicates the significance of several factors including the perceived efficacy of one's contributions, the asymmetry of contributions, the number of contributions required to provide the public good (or sustain it when it can be depleted), and the excludability of those who fail to contribute. The capacity to exclude those who do not contribute is particularly important in many decisions to participate, given the ever-present threat of free-riding in such situations (Cook and State 2017). Trust within the community of actors involved makes it easier for them to assess the trustworthiness and willingness of others to contribute. As noted above, the existence of trust is based on judgments of the trustworthiness of others, the networks that connect them, and the informal or formal rules that facilitate contributions and/or the capacity to exclude (and likely sanction) those that do not contribute. Perceptions of trustworthiness are often made on the basis of homophily, and this may have far-reaching consequences beyond the individual level. It can also affect trust at the community or neighborhood level, as has been argued by Putnam and others.

4.6   Social trust and ethnic heterogeneity

One of the factors often identified as generating high levels of generalized trust is homophily or similarity. That is, we often trust those most like ourselves more easily than we trust others who differ from us along various dimensions. For example, a mother of small children is more likely to trust another mother with small children, even one she does not know (especially when they share other traits), if the circumstances require finding someone who is likely to be trustworthy in an emergency, even if a stranger. This principle of homophily and presumed trustworthiness of those like us, while sometimes accurate, is also the basis for the success of the con artist whose expertise lies in creating an illusion of trustworthiness by their presentation of self as one who is similar or who can adopt the appearance of trustworthiness. This can be done by dress, uniform, or other means that simulate being a "trusted" person.

Recall that the 1980s serial killer Ted Bundy often dressed as a policeman to gain the trust of, and thus access to, his female victims. In many everyday ways we often base our trustworthiness judgments on appearances and other visible signals, in the absence of other reliable information. Gambetta and Hamill (2005) studied this process by interviewing taxi drivers in Belfast and New York City to discover what they identified as "signals" of presumed trustworthiness. Besides appearance, context typically mattered. For instance, was the potential client standing in front of a church or a bar? Was it late at night or during broad daylight that they were hailing a cab? Even subtle signals of group identity were important, particularly when it was hard to determine the group membership of someone when group conflict was salient. Were they Catholic or Protestant in Belfast; if not, in a familiar locale?

More generally, difference is often the source of fear and what Putnam (2007) called the tendency to "hunker down, pulling in like a turtle," exhibiting a preference for homogeneity (or homophily) that may have important consequences for social cohesion. This tendency applies to neighborhoods that are ethnically diverse, as Putnam has argued. In his view, increased ethnic diversity in the local community may lower social trust, given that those who are dissimilar are viewed as less trustworthy, and this may reduce social cohesion and limit social integration. Although some research supports this claim, indicating that generalized trust is higher in ethnically homogeneous locales (see, e.g., Knack and Keefer 1997), subsequent research proves less convincing for various reasons. In a cross-national study, Kesler and Bloemraad (2010) discovered that immigration-generated diversity only partially reduced general trust and civic participation. And Stolle, Petermann, Schmid et al. (2013) found that, although in their study neighborhood heterogeneity reduced generalized and out-group trust, interethnic contact within the neighborhood mitigated this effect to some extent (see also Stolle, Soroka and Johnston 2008). Portes and Vickstrom (2011) also challenge the claim that diversity created by immigration and ethno-racial differences reduces social cohesion, reviewing studies that provide mixed or inconsistent findings. Letki (2008), for example, reports in her study that it is low neighborhood status and not racial heterogeneity that is associated with lower levels of social cohesion. What seems to matter in understanding variations in the outcomes of this research is how trust and social cohesion are measured, where the study is conducted, and what the specific geographic boundaries are.

The latter two factors seem particularly important in explaining the differences in research findings on this topic. For example, if the research focuses on the Nordic countries, findings seem to support Putnam's original claim, depending on the geographic scope of the data available for analysis. Dinesen and Sonderskov (2015) find in their study that residential exposure to ethnic diversity lowers social trust in support of Putnam's primary claim with respect to the negative effects on social trust of integrated neighborhoods. The data these researchers explore come from the Danish registry, which has very fine-grained geographic data on the ethnic make-up of each community. They link this residential data to survey measures of trust that are collected from individuals at various times. In the data they analyze, it appears that ethnic diversity or heterogeneity at the neighborhood level is associated with lower levels of general social trust, at least in the Danish data.

Other researchers find similarly that social cohesion at the neighborhood level matters, but that the results for different geographic boundaries, particularly larger units (i.e., municipalities and countries) do not reflect the same pattern of results (Lundasen and Wollebaek 2013). As Portes and Vickstrom (2011) argue, even though social cohesion in spatially bounded neighborhoods may be reduced by ethnic diversity, other forms of solidarity, such as those that derive from extant norms and local institutions, may not decrease at all as a result. It is also the case that the findings with respect to diversity and its link to social cohesion seem to be different for different countries. Data from the United States and from the Nordic countries, for example, are more supportive of the basic claim than data from other countries, so much so that some have labeled these effects either "American exceptionalism" (van der Meer and Tolsma 2014) or "Nordic exceptionalism," depending on the case.

What is unclear is what explains the differences in the effects in various countries and why does it differ by geographic boundary? In work that examines this general set of questions, van der Meer and Tolsma (2014), among others, focus on the actual factors that may be causing these effects. They discuss four possible mechanisms (identified in the literature) that might underlie the effects of neighborhood composition on trust and social cohesion. These are anomie, homophily, group threat, and social disorganization. We have discussed homophily (preference for similarity) as the primary root cause. But van der Meer and Tolsma (2014) find little evidence for either homophily or anomie as key factors. Instead, they argue that perceived group threat that increases with the greater interethnic contact made possible by more diverse environments may be the main factor. They warn, however, that while perceived group threat may lead to distrust it "certainly does not always originate from living in heterogeneous environments" (van der Meer and Tolsma 2014: 471). They point to potential moderating effects of the degree of segregation between groups and the degree of intergroup inequality. In fact, inequality has become a central focus of much of this work.

In a study in Kenya, Buchan and Rolfe (2017) find that where ethnic fractionalization tends to exacerbate inequality it negatively affects cooperation as well as social cohesion and presumably trust. It also increases intergroup hatred and distrust. Not only group threat from those with limited access to resources, but strong views concerning the lack of fairness in income or wealth distribution may lead to distrusting attitudes that have consequences for social solidarity, typically lowering it (Fischer and Torgler 2006).

The somewhat contentious claim made by Robert Putnam (2007) that increases in ethnic heterogeneity or diversity often accompany a reduction in social trust and social cohesion at the community level continues to be debated (Sturgis, Brunton-Smith, Reid, and Allum 2011). As we have noted, past research presents somewhat mixed results with respect to the veracity of this claim based to some extent on the specific measures used, the geographic scope of the inquiry, and the countries in which the studies were conducted. As we have discovered in our review of the trust literature, clearly levels of generalized trust vary significantly by country and within countries, often by region. And the degree of ethnic homogeneity varies partly as a result of history as well as the continuing, and recently increasing, patterns of immigration and the resettlement of refugees affecting populations all over the world. Terrorism, internal conflicts, war, political uncertainty and now, more than ever, the effects of climate change and weather extremes are fueling this flood of relocation movements. But what is it about ethnic diversity that matters? And does it vary by the measure of trust that is used?

Here we present a brief summary of a recent review of more research across countries based on an in-depth meta-analysis of the existing findings recently published in the *Annual Review of Political Science*. Dinesen, Schaeffer, and Sonderskov (2020) report that, overall, they find a negative correlation between ethnic diversity and social trust that "is stronger for trust in neighbors and when ethnic diversity is measured more locally." Their review covers over 1,000 estimates of this effect in the 87 studies they included in their meta-analysis of reported findings. We go into a bit more detail in their excellent review here to get a sense of the actual findings and the reasons for conflicting results. What is most useful about this review is that they separate the analyses by the type of trust involved – trust of neighbors, generalized trust (in strangers), trust within groups, and trust of those considered outsiders. All have been the focus of some research.

The two most relevant for our focus is generalized trust (key to this chapter) and trust in neighbors. As the authors note (Dinesen et al. 2020: 452): "a plausible interpretation of the stronger relationship between ethnic diversity and trust in neighbors [which they find] is that exposure to ethnically dissimilar others is a stronger and more directly relevant cue in neighbors than is trust in other people in general," a much weaker effect in the studies reviewed. They also discover in this vein that context matters, and that ethnic diversity has a stronger association with social trust when it is closer to home, that is in the neighborhood more so than in the region or country (Dinesen et al. 2020: 453, Figure 3). Thus, at the local level, it appears that contact matters, though it seems to have less effect than might be expected as we widen the geographic lens. The authors conclude with an important disclaimer about the existence of a negative association between ethnic diversity (or fragmentation) and social trust, either in neighbors or more generally. Their findings, though they support a negative association, do not justify the "apocalyptic claims regarding the severe threat of ethnic diversity for social trust in contemporary societies" (Dinesen et al. 2020: 457). Other factors contribute to weakening this threat, including well-functioning government as well as an increase in segregated living conditions in some regions and countries. (See Dinesen et al. 2020 for the details of their analysis and conclusions concerning future explorations of causality and related policy implications.) Recent work emphasizes the role that inequality (in both wealth and income) has in reducing generalized trust and social cohesion. Here we present some data on the United States.

4.7   Inequality and generalized trust

It appears that research in several disciplines indicates that inequality in a society is directly related to social trust. As noted earlier in this chapter, those societies with lower levels of inequality (typically income inequality) show up in cross-country comparisons as having higher levels of general social trust (Jordahl 2009). Conversely, societies with the highest

Gini coefficients, a standard measure of income inequality, are typically those with the lowest levels of generalized trust. The higher the Gini coefficient, the greater the income inequality. A comparison of Norway and Denmark with Brazil and South Africa is illustrative of this fact. According to Newton (2007: 356), "national wealth (a simple measure of GDP per capita) and income inequality are associated with high trust. It seems that for poor countries it is wealth that matters, but for rich countries it is income inequality that matters" with respect to social trust. Few studies include wealth inequality; most focus on income.

The decline in social trust in individuals over time in the United States may be related to the increasing wealth inequality characteristic of more recent decades. Inequality reduces social similarity across the socio-economic divide and typically lowers the frequency of cross-cutting social ties that may ameliorate such differences (e.g., Clark 2015). Inequality has both direct and indirect effects in lowering trust in others. Uslaner and Brown (2005) find that the strongest predictor of trust in the U.S.A. (as well as cross-nationally) is economic inequality, and it works through its effects on social trust in two ways. "First, high levels of inequality lead to less optimism for the future" and, second, where there is a high degree of inequality "people in different economic strata will be less likely to have a sense of shared fate" (Uslaner and Brown 2005: 870). These two factors lower trust and lead to division.

Figure 4.5 includes a simple depiction of the recent decades in which there has been a steep increase in wealth inequality in the United States exacerbating the gap between those at the bottom of the wealth gradient and those in the top tier prior to the coronavirus pandemic. Figure 4.6 presents the income gaps. These gaps are likely to increase post-pandemic, given the differential impact of Covid-19 on those with the fewest resources to weather the storm. Other differential effects, especially on children and their access to education, may be long-lasting, resulting in continued intergenerational deprivation and further increases in income and wealth gaps and their stability over time.

As many researchers have pointed out in a variety of contexts, inequality is also linked to democratization. Houle (2009: 591, cited in Letki 2018: 347) concludes that "inequality increases the probability of backsliding from democracy to dictatorship" and there are a number of examples of this process. It is also the case that "social structure polarizes as

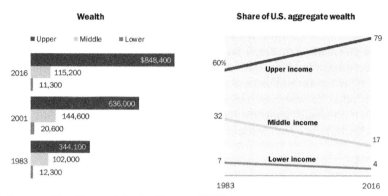

Source: Pew Research Center (January 2020).

Figure 4.5   Wealth gaps in the United States 1983–2016

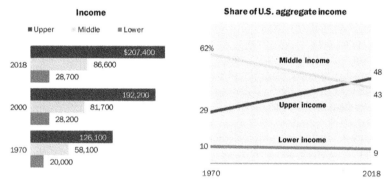

Source: Pew Research Center (January 2020).

Figure 4.6   Income gaps in the United States 1970–2018

inequalities grow, which breeds in-group trust at the expense of generalized trust and solidarity" (Letki 2018: 347). In some ways this is what has been occurring in the United States as political parties deepen the divide between Republicans and Democrats, increasing polarization in the context of a more autocratic leader as president (Trump, 2016–20) and widespread inequality, as pictured above in Figures 4.5 and 4.6. Commenting on other countries in which inequality has interfered with the transition to democracy or has been a result of such a transition, Letki (2018: 348) suggests that "Growing distances between socioeconomic groups reduced their sense of shared goals and norms, which thus had a negative impact on generalized trust (Uslaner 2008b)." Instead, existing trust networks within groups were strengthened and distrust of those "outside" the group increased. The inequality exacerbated the tendency to engage in exchanges with those in one's close network and consolidated what Letki calls "the short radius of homophily based trust networks" (Letki 2018: 348). It also reduced trust in the emerging proto-democratic institutions and stymied efforts to reform them. And these factors varied in significance in different locales.

4.8   Cross-country comparisons

Data from various sources provide a window into the variation across countries in their levels of general social trust or the extent to which individuals in that country tend to trust others in their society in response to questions such as: "Generally speaking, would you say most people can be trusted or that you can't be too careful in dealing with people?" Such questions, while heavily criticized, have been included for some time in a number of surveys including the GSS in the United States as well as the WVS. Criticisms focus on the wording of the question, specifically variations in the meaning and interpretations of "most" people, and the double-barreled nature of the question (Sturgis and Smith 2010; Robbins 2019). Other groups have developed and administered their own surveys in various countries such as the Edelman Trust Barometer (focusing mainly on institutional trust) and a number of Pew Foundation surveys (referenced above). We have already referred to these sources of data in earlier chapters. Here we comment briefly on factors that researchers have associated with the cross-country variations in general social trust.

Clearly, the degree of inequality in the society, as described above, is one major factor. In addition, a number of studies have focused on ethno-racial differences within countries in generalized trust (for an overview, see Wilkes and Wu, 2018) and these differences may be exacerbated by inequality. More generally, Halpern (2005: 281) argues that economic inequality is a "close correlate of low social capital, indicating that a stretching of the socioeconomic fabric tends to undermine the common ground on which much social capital is built," particularly trust. We present some data on country variations in levels of general social

Table 4.1   Country variations in levels of general social trust

Denmark	67
Sweden	66
Norway	65
China	56
Japan	43
India	41
Australia	40
Canada	39
Egypt	38
Spain	36
USA	36
Austria	34
Italy	33
UK	30
S. Korea	27
Nigeria	26
Israel	24
Greece	24
Russia	24
Chile	23
Hungary	22
Mexico	21
Poland	19
Singapore	17
Bosnia	16
Venezuela	16
Argentina	16
S. Africa	12
Algeria	11

Denmark	67
Colombia	11
Peru	11
Romania	10
Uganda	8
Tanzania	8
Brazil	3

Source: WVS (Wave IV, 1999–2000).

trust from a WVS in Table 4.1. The entries are the percentage of the adult population in each country (in the sample) who say that "most people can be trusted." The more complete data table is included in Newton (2007). We include just a few of the countries for reference here. Over time, while there are slight increases and decreases in level of social trust, these percentages remain somewhat stable, reflecting both historical trends and the limits to structural change.

Groups within a society may differ in their levels of general trust and the reasons behind it. What Wilkes and Wu (2018: 237) conclude from their review of relevant studies is that: "Irrespective of how minority is defined, and irrespective of the country considered, respondents who identify as an ethnic minority have lower generalized trust than respondents who do not." The same pattern does not emerge with respect to political trust that focuses on institutions and their performance more than on individuals in the society. With respect to political trust, Wilkes and Wu (2018: 240) find that ethnic minorities actually tend to have higher political trust than those who are native-born, with the exception of black Americans who have lower political trust than white Americans, and this pattern has been consistent over time (Simpson, McCrimmon, and Irwin 2007; Smith 2010). The attitudes of African Americans appear to be based on a deep distrust of the political system and its long-standing failures to address structural racism in the United States, as well as some well-founded distrust of other institutions, including the medical establishment, that have failed them for the same reason. In other countries for which such data exist, factors such as political efficacy and the performance of government matter with respect to level of corruption and reduced confidence in procedural fairness and representativeness where it applies.

Crime is another arena in which aspects of social capital have been argued to have significant effects, particularly the level of social trust at the community level. Interestingly, variations in crime rates (e.g., homicides) have been viewed as an important indicator of local social capital, especially the existence of social trust.

4.9   Social capital and crime

In a number of studies following the publication of Putnam's work, researchers have investigated the linkages between aspects of social capital and crime, a major concern for citizens and local government alike. We mentioned findings related to neighborhood network density and criminal activities in Chapter 2. Here we focus on the role of social trust and crime. Kennedy, Kawachi, Prothrow-Stith, Lochner, and Gupta (1998), for example, found that income inequality was associated with crime (homicide and other violent acts) and this relationship was mediated by social capital – specifically, levels of social trust and membership in various local groups and associations. The income inequality lowered social trust, as we have found in other studies not focused on crime as the key outcome (e.g., in the study of corruption).

In related research, Messner, Baumer, and Rosenfeld (2004) report similar findings with respect to social trust and homicide, but find no association with other aspects of social capital. Specifically, they find that social trust is negatively associated with rates of homicide, that is, lower trust is linked with an increase in homicides. They also find that higher levels of social activism are positively linked to homicide rates, meaning an increase in activism is associated with more homicides. The disorder that often accompanies such events may be a key factor in explaining this connection. It appears that, in many domains of behavior, social capital matters, but findings are often inconsistent, as we have noted throughout this book, due to lack of clarity and differences in the specific aspect of social capital that is the focus of investigation, how it is measured, and the quality of the data available at both the individual and the aggregate levels (see Section 1.3 in Chapter 1 on conceptual and measurement issues). We have tried to separate the various dimensions of social capital to offer some clarity about what exactly is being investigated.

4.10 Particularized trust

The bulk of this chapter has focused attention on social trust (or generalized trust) and its societal effects in the tradition of Putnam's work on social capital and civil society, mainly addressing the community- and broad societal-level impacts. But trust between individuals known to each other, referred to in the literature as particularized trust, is also the focus of decades of research. Cook, Hardin, and Levi (2005), among others, talk about trust as relational, meaning that more than a psychological attitude that we possess as being trusting or not (cf., Rotter 1971, 1980), trust is fundamentally a characteristic of a relationship between individuals (or other entities). The general defining feature is represented as A trusts B with respect to X, indicating that actor A trusts actor (or entity) B with respect to some domain of activity X (or thing). So, I might trust you with respect to taking care of my child, but not with respect to handling my finances (or vice versa). For Hardin (2002, and subsequently Cook, Hardin, and Levi 2005), this occurs when A believes that B's interests encapsulate or include her own; thus she can accept vulnerability with respect to engaging with B in some domain of action or more generally, when the range of actions is quite broad.

This "encapsulated interest" view of trust makes it clear that while there is uncertainty in any act of trust and typically some vulnerability or risk, it is also possible to assess the level of risk involved based on beliefs about B's trustworthiness with respect to X. This typically includes an assessment of B's past actions involving actor A (i.e., the shadow of the past), the probability of future interactions (i.e., the shadow of the future), and B's reputation to the extent that it can be known, not to mention his or her capabilities, which should be a component of the reputational judgment of trustworthiness.

The important feature of this view of trust is that it is relational and thus captures the heart of what we often mean when we say we trust someone else. It is more of a sociological view of trust (see also Cook 2005). In addition, we may have a psychological disposition to trust or to be a trusting person, based in part on early life experiences, but this is not sufficient to explain the kind of trust that emerges and/or persists in social relationships. Although certainly we may sometimes initially enter relationships as a trusting person, we may learn that we have misplaced our trust and that the one we have trusted is not trustworthy. This is the version of trust and sometimes the betrayal of trust that we find in interpersonal relationships, often with those closest to us. It is also why the betrayal of trust can be so painful particularly in long-term relationships. We believed in someone's trustworthiness with respect to us, only to be deeply disappointed. Many compelling novels are based on such betrayals.

In contexts in which there is great risk and uncertainty, networks of friends, family, and colleagues often form in order to limit risk and to gain some degree of certainty in order to obtain support and needed resources, especially under conditions of scarcity. In Eastern European countries after the fall of communism, people tell tales of finding out that a once-trusted colleague or friend had "turned them in" for illegal activities under the former communist regime. In fact, the regime relied on locals to monitor and report such activities and they were rewarded for it. Such trust networks (discussed to some extent in Chapter 2) remain strong in these settings as they provide a modicum of safety in an otherwise exploitive environment, even if they are occasionally breached.

As we note earlier in this chapter, Radaev (2004) writes about such networks in Russia where reliance on even close relatives may not be enough to secure a transaction, given the widespread lack of any form of reliable institutional backing for failed contracts. The situation has not changed much in Russia in the ensuing decades. The downside of reliance on relatively small trust networks for significant transactions is the opportunity cost of not attempting to broaden one's access to resources from those outside the network. While these trust networks made exchange possible under the circumstances, they may have retarded the transition to a more open economy in which transactions can occur among strangers, typically because they have recourse to some form of institutional backing in the case of betrayal or failure to abide by contractual terms. This is a relatively clear case in which bounded networks involving only particularized trust inhibited economic development with implications much broader than just the economic realm, in support of Fukuyama's (1995) central claim.

While there is a large literature on particularized trust, primarily in psychology and sociology, in this chapter we have focused more on generalized social trust, given its link to arguments about the macro-level effects of this form of social capital, especially in the economic and political domains. Schilke, Reimann, and Cook (2021) suggest that we should move beyond treating particularized and generalized trust as a dichotomy and instead view them as two ends of a continuum, conceiving of a "radius of trust" that varies from trust in individuals to groups and larger aggregates of people or organizations, including many who are anonymous, as is the case with most institutions. In their formulation, groups or categories of people can be the object of trust at the mid-scale and we have evidence of the group-level trust that exists in many settings. This is also the basis for much of the research on trust and ethnic heterogeneity involving intergroup relations that we have reviewed above.

What we don't have yet is a clear theoretical or empirical view of how particularistic and generalized trust are connected, if at all. Some would argue that widespread particularistic trust among individuals leads to higher levels of generalized trust, as if trusting many specific individuals allows us to reach out and trust strangers as well. Others argue that too much particularistic trust in a society hinders the emergence of more generalized trust, extending beyond the confines of the familiar. Often group- or kin-based trust networks are tight knit, as we have noted, and exclude those outside their boundaries, increasing distrust rather than generating trust of strangers. On this view they are clearly negatively associated.

4.11 Beyond trust: understanding its limitations

The literature on social capital and trust, more specifically, has drawn attention to the many ways in which social order is fragile. Too much reliance on the vagaries of our capacity to trust others and to accurately assess the trustworthiness not only of those individuals but also the groups, organizations, networks, and institutions of which they are a part would be naïve to say the least. As Cook, Hardin, and Levi (2005) have argued, trust alone cannot bear the weight of producing cooperation, collective action for the public good, and social order more generally, in large societies. Even in small-scale societies of the past in which individuals were fairly well known to one another, trust, when it existed, was bolstered by the presence of communal norms and the sanctions that go along with them, if not some version of a local authority granted the duty of monitoring compliance. In some of the social science work on trust, its role in society has been somewhat exaggerated. It is one mechanism for securing cooperation, but there are alternatives, many of which are also evolving to meet the challenges of a more complex, risk-ridden and uncertain world.

Ironically, trust is typically needed even more under such circumstances, but it can also be hard won when the risk of exploitation is ever present.

Understanding the limits of trust is important. We have already written about the downsides of closed or bounded trust networks and the potential for a negative association between within group trust and trust of "outsiders." And trusting when it is not warranted is always a problem. But there are mechanisms often put in place to reduce the reliance on trust alone. For example, elements of organizational structure exist that support reliability and help to reduce the possibility of exploitation. This category includes monitoring mechanisms as well as certain types of management compensation schemes that reward trustworthiness, creating incentives compatible with such behavior. Incentives are sometimes put in place to make exploitive behavior costly, even entailing termination of employment or loss of associational membership and access to the resources entailed. Many organizations and even associations have codes of conduct that limit bad behavior, short of legal remedies that may additionally be available in many circumstances. This depends, of course, on the viability and effectiveness of the existing legal institutions. Trust is easier to produce and sustain in the presence of reliable institutional backing, since it is risk-limited against the most egregious forms of exploitation.

Other alternatives to reliance on trust are explored in depth in Cook, Hardin, and Levi (2005). Mechanisms such as the use of self-regulation schemes in professional associations (e.g., the American Medical Association), as well as reputational mechanisms that make violations of trust costly, represent examples. Once a reputation is sullied it is hard to repair. There is a reason that reputation schemes have become the coin of the realm in the world of Internet interactions and transactions. Institutionalized enforcement strategies to limit the vulnerability of the parties to an exchange also form a key component of the kind of institutional backing that constrains the vulnerability inherent in actions based solely on trust (or, more precisely, presumed trustworthiness).

In their book *Cooperation without Trust?*, Cook, Hardin, and Levi (2005) explore many of the implications of the use of these and other mechanisms for securing trustworthiness in the production of social order at various levels, from the interpersonal realm of particularized trust to the macro level involving associations, organizations, and institutions that requires more general trust. At larger scales, reliance on trust is rarely sufficient partly because it is impossible to fully assess trustworthiness accurately. Cultures of trust may even restrict the information that is allowed to be circulated and cultures of distrust are rife with misinformation. In addition, when distrust is the norm, it forms a kind of self-fulfilling prophecy or vicious cycle in which distrust breeds more and more distrust over time and across boundaries. Breaking out of these vicious cycles, whether in interpersonal relations, organizations, or larger social entities like communities or even nation states, has proven difficult.

Note

1. "The final four institutions deal mostly with learning and knowledge. On average they have had higher ratings than the economic, governmental, and media groups, but with one exception have shown decline over time ... The exception is that confidence in the Scientific Community has varied little and shown no decline. The 2012 rating of 39.7% is very close to the long-term average of 40.2%. Confidence in Education has decreased over time from a high of 49.0% in 1974 to low points of 23.7% in 1993–1996 and 25.6% in 2012. Confidence in Medicine dropped from 61.0% in 1974 to a low of 37.5% in 2002–2004. In 2012, it was at its third lowest point with 38.9%. Confidence in Organized Religion has had a general decline and has fallen in response to religious scandals. It decreased from a high of 44.5% in 1974 to a low of 20.5% in 1988 during the televangelist scandals, rebounded to 27.6% in 2000 before plummeting to a record low of 18.9% during the Catholic sex-abuse scandals. It came back up somewhat to 24.1% in 2006 before slipping to 19.9% in 2008–2012" (Smith and Son 2013, GSS report from NORC).

References

Arrow, Kenneth (1974). *The Limits of Organization*. New York: Norton.
Bjornskov, Christian (2018). "Social Trust and Economic Growth." Pp. 535–55 in Eric M. Uslaner (ed.), *The Oxford Handbook of Social and Political Trust*. New York: Oxford University Press.
Buchan, Nancy and Robert Rolfe (2017). "The Influence of Globalization and Ethnic Fractionalization on Cooperation and Trust in Kenya." Pp. 215–36 in Paul A.M. van Lange, Bettina Rockenbach, and Toshio Yamagishi (eds.), *Trust in Social Dilemmas*. New York: Oxford University Press.
Clark, April K. (2015). "Rethinking the Decline in Social Capital." *American Politics Research* 43(4): 560–601.

Coleman, James S. (1988). "Social Capital in the Creation of Human Capital." *American Journal of Sociology* 94: S95–S120.

Cook, Karen S. (2005). "Networks, Norms and Trust: The Social Psychology of Social Capital." *Social Psychology Quarterly* 68: 4–14.

Cook, Karen S. and Bogdan State (2017). "Trust and Social Dilemmas." Pp. 9–30 in Paul A.M. van Lange, Bettina Rockenbach, and Toshio Yamagishi (eds.), *Trust in Social Dilemmas*. New York: Oxford University Press.

Cook, Karen S., Russell Hardin, and Margaret Levi (2005). *Cooperation Without Trust?* New York: Russell Sage Foundation.

Dinesen, Peter Thisted and Kim Mannemar Sonderskov (2015). "Ethnic Diversity and Social Trust: Evidence from the Micro-Context." *American Sociological Review* 80: 550–73.

Dinesen, Peter Thisted, Merlin Schaeffer, and Kim Mannemar Sonderskov (2020). "Ethnic Diversity and Social Trust: A Narrative and Meta-Analytical Review" *Annual Review of Political Science* 23: 441–65.

Ermisch, J. and Diego Gambetta (2010). "Do Strong Family Ties Inhibit Trust?" *Journal of Economic Behavior and Organization* 75: 365–76.

Fischer, J.A. and B. Torgler (2006). "The Effect of Relative Income Position on Social Capital." *Economics Bulletin* 26(4): 1–20.

Fukuyama, Frances (1995). *Trust: The Social Virtues and the Creation of Prosperity*. New York: Penguin.

Gambetta, Diego (1988). "Mafia: The Price of Distrust." Pp. 158–75 in Diego Gambetta (ed.), *Trust: Making and Breaking Cooperative Relations*. London: Basil Blackwell.

Gambetta, Diego and Heather Hamill (2005). *Streetwise: How Taxi Drivers Establish Their Customers' Trustworthiness?* New York: Russell Sage Foundation.

Halpern, David (2005). *Social Capital*. Cambridge: Polity Press.

Hardin, Russell (2002). *Trust and Trustworthiness*. New York: Russell Sage Foundation.

Houle, Christian (2009). "Inequality and Democracy: Why Inequality Harms Consolidation but Does Not Affect Democratization." *World Politics* 61(4): 589–622.

Howard, Marc Morje (2003). *The Weakness of Civil Society in Post-Communist Europe*. Cambridge: Cambridge University Press.

Jordahl, Henrik (2009). "Economic Inequality." Pp. 323–36 in Gert Tinggaard Svendsen and Gunnar Lind Haase Svendsen (eds.), *Handbook of Social Capital: The Troika of Sociology, Political Science and Economics*. Cheltenham, UK and Northampton, MA, USA: Edward Elgar Publishing.

Keele, Luke J. (2007). "Social Capital and the Dynamics of Trust in Government." *American Journal of Political Science* 51(2): 241–54.

Kennedy, Bruce P., Ichiro Kawachi, Deborah Prothrow-Stith, Kimberly Lochner, and Vanita Gupta (1998). "Social Capital, Income Inequality, and Firearm Violent Crime." *Social Science & Medicine* 47(1): 7–17.

Kesler C. and I. Bloemraad (2010). "Does Immigration Erode Social Capital? The Conditional Effects of Immigration-Generated Diversity on Trust, Membership and Participation across 19 Countries, 1981–2000." *Canadian Journal of Political Science* 43(2): 319–47.

Knack, Stephen and Philip Keefer (1997). "Does Social Capital Have an Economic Payoff? A Cross-Country Investigation." *Quarterly Journal of Economics* 112(4): 1251–88.

Kornai, Janos (1996). "Paying the Bill for Goulash Communism: Hungarian Development and Macro Stabilization in a Political Economy Perspective." *Social Research* 63: 943–1040.

La Porta, R., F. Lopez-de-Salinas, A. Shleifer, and R.W. Vishny (1997). "Trust in Large Organizations." *American Economic Review* 87: 333–8.

Letki, Natalia (2004). "Socialization for Participation? Trust, Membership, and Democratization in East-Central Europe." *Political Research Quarterly* 57(4): 665–79.

Letki, Natalia (2006). "Investigating the Roots of Civic Morality: Trust Social Capital and Institutional Performance." *Political Behavior* 28(4): 305–25.

Letki, Natalia (2008). "Does Diversity Erode Social Capital? Social Capital and Race in British Neighbourhoods." *Political Studies* 56(1): 99–126.

Letki, Natalia (2018). "Trust in Newly Democratic Regimes." Pp. 336–56 in Eric M. Uslaner (ed.), *The Oxford Handbook of Social and Political Trust*. Oxford: Oxford University Press.

Levi, Margaret (1988). *Of Revenue and Rule*. Berkeley: University of California Press.

Levi, Margaret (1997). *Consent, Dissent and Patriotism*. New York: Cambridge University Press.

Levi, Margaret (1998). "A State of Trust." Pp. 77–101 in Valerie Braithwaite and Margaret Levi (eds.), *Trust and Governance*. New York: Russell Sage Foundation.

Levi, Margaret and Laura Stoker (2000). "Political Trust and Trustworthiness." *Annual Review of Political Science* 3: 475–507.

Lundasen, Susanne W. and Dag Wollebaek (2013). "Diversity and Community Trust in Swedish Local Communities." *Journal of Elections, Public Opinion and Parties* 23(3): 299–321.

Messner, Steven F., Eric P. Baumer, and Richard Rosenfeld (2004). "Dimensions of Social Capital and Rates of Criminal Homicide." *American Sociological Review* 69(6): 882–903.

Montinola, Gabriela (2004). "Corruption, Distrust, and the Deterioration of the Rule of Law." Pp. 298–323 in Russell Hardin (ed.), *Distrust*. New York: Russell Sage Foundation.

Newton, Kenneth (2007). "Social and Political Trust." Pp. 342–61 in Russell J. Dalton and Hans-Dieter Klingeman (eds.), *The Oxford Handbook of Political Behavior*. Oxford: Oxford University Press.

Ostrom, Elinor (2003). "Toward a Behavioral Theory Linking Trust, Reciprocity and Reputation." Pp. 19–79 in Elinor Ostrom and James Walker (eds.), *Trust & Reciprocity: Interdisciplinary Lessons from Experimental Research*. New York: Russell Sage Foundation.

Ostrom, Elinor and T.K. Ahn (2009). "The Meaning of Social Capital and Its Link to Collective Action." Pp. 17–35 in Gert Tinggaard Svendsen and Gunnar Lind Haase Svendsen (eds.), *Handbook of Social Capital: The Troika of Sociology, Political Science and Economics*. Cheltenham, UK and Northampton, MA, USA: Edward Elgar Publishing.

Paldam, Martin (2009). "The Macro Perspective on Generalized Trust." Pp. 354–78 in Gert Tinggaard Svendsen and Gunnar Lind Haase (eds.), *Handbook of Social Capital: The Troika of Sociology, Political Science and Economics.* Cheltenham, UK and Northampton, MA, USA: Edward Elgar Publishing.

Pew Research Center (2019). "Why Americans Don't Fully Trust Many Who Hold Positions of Power and Responsibility." https://www.pewresearch.org/politics/2019/09/19/where-public-confidence-stands-about-eight-groups-that-have-positions-of-power-and-responsibility/.

Pew Research Center (2020). "Most Americans Say There Is Too Much Economic Inequality in the U.S., but Fewer Than Half Call It a Top Priority" January 9, https://www.pewresearch.org/social-trends/2020/01/09/most-americans-say-there-is-too-much-economic-inequality-in-the-u-s-but-fewer-than-half-call-it-a-top-priority/.

Portes, Alejandro (1998). "Social Capital: Its Origins and Applications in Modern Sociology." *Annual Review of Sociology* 24: 1–24.

Portes, Alejandro and Erik Vickstrom (2011). "Diversity, Social Capital and Cohesion." *Annual Review of Sociology* 37: 461–79.

Putnam, Robert D. (2000). *Bowling Alone: The Collapse and Revival of American Community.* New York: Simon & Schuster.

Putnam, Robert D. (2007). "E Pluribus Unum: Diversity and Community in the Twenty-First Century." *Scandinavian Political Studies*, 30(2): 137–74.

Putnam, Robert D. (2020). *The Upswing: How America Came Together a Century Ago and How We Can Do It Again.* New York: Simon & Schuster.

Putnam, Robert D., R. Leonardi, and R. Nanetti (1993). *Making Democracies Work: Civic Traditions in Modern Italy.* Princeton, NJ: Princeton University Press.

Radaev, Vadim (2004). "How Trust is Established in Economic Relationships when Institutions and Individuals are Not Trustworthy: The Case of Russia." Pp. 91–110 in Janos Kornai, Bo Rothstein, and Susan Rose-Ackerman (eds.), *Creating Social Trust in Post-Socialist Transition.* New York: Palgrave Macmillan.

Robbins, Blaine G. (2019). "Measuring Generalized Trust: Two New Approaches." *Sociological Methods & Research*: 1–52. https://doi.org/10.1177/0049124119852371.

Rotter, J.B. (1971). "Generalized Expectancies for Interpersonal Trust." *American Psychologist* 26: 443–52.

Rotter, J.B. (1980). "Interpersonal Trust, Trustworthiness, and Gullibility." *American Psychologist* 35: 1–7.

Schilke, Oliver, Martin Reimann, and Karen S. Cook (2021). "Trust in Social Relations." *Annual Review of Sociology* 47: 239–59.

Simpson, B., T. McCrimmon, and K. Irwin (2007). "Are Blacks Really Less Trusting than Whites? Revisiting the Race and Trust Question." *Social Forces* 86: 525–52.

Smith, Sandra S. (2010). "Race and Trust." *Annual Review of Sociology* 36: 453–65.

Smith, Tom W. and Jaesok Son (2013). *General Social Survey 2012 Final Report: Trends in Public Attitudes about Confidence in Institutions.* Chicago: NORC.

Stolle, Dietlind (2007). "Social Capital." Pp. 655–74 in Russell J. Dalton and Hans-Dieter Klingemann (eds.), *The Oxford Handbook of Political Behavior*. Oxford: Oxford University Press.

Stolle, D., S. Soroka, and R. Johnston (2008). "When Does Diversity Erode Trust: Neighborhood Diversity, Interpersonal Trust and the Mediating Effect of Social Interactions." *Political Studies* 56(1): 57–75.

Stolle, Dietlind, Soren Petermann, Katharina Schmid, Karen Schonwalder, Miles Hewstone, Steven Vertovec, Thomas Schmitt, and Joe Heywood (2013). "Immigrant-Related Diversity and Trust in German Cities: Trust and the Role of Intergroup Contact." *Journal of Elections, Public Opinion and Parties* 23(3): 279–98.

Sturgis, Patrick and Patten Smith (2010). "Assessing the Validity of Generalized Trust Questions: What Kind of Trust Are We Measuring?" *International Journal of Public Opinion Research* 22(1): 74–92.

Sturgis, Patrick, Ian Brunton-Smith, Sanne Reid, and Nick Allum (2011). "Does Ethnic Diversity Erode Trust?: Putnam's 'Hunkering Down' Thesis Reconsidered." *British Journal of Political Science* 41(1): 57–82.

Tarrow, Sidney (1996). "Making Social Science Work Across Space and Time: A Critical Reflection on Robert Putnam's *Making Democracy Work*." *American Political Science Review* 90(2): 389–97.

Uslaner, Eric M. (2003). "Trust and Civic Engagement in East and West." Pp. 81–94 in G. Badescu and E. Uslaner (eds.), *Social Capital and the Transition to Democracy*. London: Routledge.

Uslaner, Eric M. (2008a). "Where You Stand Depends upon Where your Grandparents Sat: The Inheritability of Generalized Trust." *Public Opinion Quarterly* 72: 725–40.

Uslaner, Eric M. (2008b). *Corruption, Inequality, and the Rule of Law*. New York: Cambridge University Press.

Uslaner, Eric M. (2009). "Corruption." Pp. 127–42 in Gert Tinggaard Svendsen and Gunnar Lind Haase (eds.), *Handbook of Social Capital: The Troika of Sociology, Political Science and Economics*. Cheltenham, UK and Northampton, MA, USA: Edward Elgar Publishing.

Uslaner, Eric M. and Mitchell Brown (2005). "Inequality, Trust and Civic Engagement." *American Politics Research* 33(6): 868–94.

Van der Meer, T. and V. Tolsma (2014). "Ethnic Diversity and Its Effects on Social Cohesion." *Annual Review of Sociology* 40: 459–78.

Van Lange, Paul A.M., Daniel Balliet, Craig D. Parks, and Mark Van Vugt (2014). *Social Dilemmas: The Psychology of Human Cooperation*. Oxford: Oxford University Press.

Wilkes, Rima and Cary Wu (2018). "Trust and Minority Groups." Pp. 231–50 in Eric M. Uslaner (ed.), *The Oxford Handbook of Social and Political Trust*. Oxford: Oxford University Press.

WVS (2020). Inglehart, R., Haerpfer, C., Moreno, A., Welzel, C., Kizilova, K., Diez-Medrano J., M. Lagos, P. Norris, E. Ponarin & B. Puranen et al. (eds.). World Values Survey: All Rounds – Country-Pooled Datafile. Madrid, Spain & Vienna, Austria: JD Systems Institute & WVSA Secretariat. http://www.worldvaluessurvey.org/WVSDocumentationWVL.jsp.

You, J.S. (2015). *Democracy, Inequality and Corruption: Korea, Taiwan and the Philippines Compared*. Cambridge: Cambridge University Press.

You, J.S. (2018). "Trust and Corruption." Pp. 474–96 in Eric M. Uslaner (ed.), *The Oxford Handbook of Social and Political Trust*. Oxford: Oxford University Press.

Zak, Paul and Stephen Knack (2001). "Trust and Growth." *Economic Journal* 3: 295–321.

5 Conclusions and the path forward

> Nowhere is the need to restore connectedness, trust and civic engagement clearer than in the now empty forums of our democracy.
>
> (Putnam 2000: 412)

In his most recent book, *The Upswing: How America Came Together a Century Ago and How We Can Do It Again*, Putnam presents another sweeping account of trends related to social capital over time. He makes the claim that "Between the mid-1960s and today ... we have been experiencing *declining* economic equality, the *deterioration* of compromise in the public square, a *fraying* social fabric and a *descent* into cultural narcissism" (Putnam 2020: 11). The role of changes in what we refer to as the elements of social capital (networks, norms, and trust) are clearly implicated in these trends. Taking a historically broader view, Robert Putnam, who popularized the use of the term social capital, takes us on a journey to find the time in the past when we as a nation were able to turn the tide on similar negative trends and to identify the forces that might move us back on a path toward creating a "we" not just an "I" culture that is more inclusive and less divisive. This book is a logical extension of his earlier work, which placed emphasis on declining social capital and the worrisome demise of aspects of civil society at the dawn of the twenty-first century.

In this volume we have revisited some of his previous work on social capital (and the research that came after) that laid the groundwork for several of the subsequent books written by Putnam (or co-authored), including: *Our Kids: The American Dream in Crisis* (2016), *American Grace: How Religion Divides and Unites Us* (2010), *and Better Together: Restoring the American Community* (2007), in addition to the most recent book, *The Upswing* (2020). He has become a major voice in the current period, pushing us to evaluate where we are as a nation, how we got here, and how we can fix what is troubling societies around the globe, but most notably here at home in the United States. Of particular concern is the future of democracy. Putnam is not alone in this fear. In his view, if we came together once before as a country after the Gilded Age to create a more equal society in which many prospered (but see the chapters in *Upswing* on race and gender), we can do it again. The real challenge before us is: *can we*? And what are the implications for governance if we can't?

Research on the various elements of social capital lends some clues. It also raises more questions that we need answers to from social science as well as policy scholars. In this chapter, after a brief reprise, we identify some of the topics to be addressed in future research and policymaking efforts. Given that this book is just an introduction to a vast literature it should be made clear that we have only been able to scratch the surface of the relevant research, reviews, and related policy papers on a range of perplexing problems linked to networks, norms, and trust facing us as a nation and as a member of the global community.

5.1   Networks

Networks form the core component of social capital, as I have argued, primarily because this is the key source of what is often referred to as social capital, defined as the networks that provide the connections to the resources and services we need and value highly, provided by others. It is the social connections we have to others, to groups, to organizations and institutions that open doors for us and form a basis for social cohesion. The lack of such connections denies us access. Much of the inequality in any society (democratic or not) is produced by either the lack of access or its abundance for some and not others. In fact, as inequality increases, threats to democratic regimes (as well as autocracies) rise and social trust declines. This is most certainly the case in the United States, as we have discussed in Chapters 2 and 4.

The networks Putnam emphasized included primarily those that connect us through engagement with various social and political associations, central to his view of the roots of civil society and the "now empty forums of democracy." Others define civil society in broader terms, focusing more on new forms of association (including those that are global) and institutional involvement (Cohen 1999). Critics also argue that it is not at all clear whether participation in civil society of the type Putnam discusses in his work helps create the kind of generalized social trust needed to support collective action involving those outside the social bonds created by such participation. That is, it remains to be determined whether what emerges is particularized trust, limited in scope, which may undermine generalized trust instead. As Uslaner (e.g., 1999) has argued, there is typically a negative correlation between particularized trust and generalized trust. Cohen (1999) criticizes Putnam for not spelling out how the trust produced between people in voluntary associations generalizes. She asks, "How does intragroup trust become trust of strangers outside the group?" (Cohen 1999: 219–20). It could instead foster exclusion, intolerance, or even distrust of those on the outside.

For a more prosperous society, interaction with strangers is required, moving beyond the networks occupied by those we know – close friends and family. This is the basic argument behind the role of general social trust in increased investments and economic growth in market economies (Fukuyama 1995; Knack and Keefer 1997). Interactions with strangers for exchange and trade fuel economies, but such interactions must be backed by network-based reciprocity and eventual trustworthiness, or by institutions in which we have confidence. Otherwise, we retreat into our closed networks of trusted contacts, typically reducing opportunity (Cook, Rice, and Gerbasi 2004). This is one of the main theses in Fukuyama's (1995) cross-cultural analysis of social trust in relation to economic growth. Moving beyond the familiar to take advantage of resources offered in other network domains is also key to immigrant integration in various cultures and a source of economic opportunity. Closed networks, while they facilitate initial adaptation to a new society, may restrict access to resources that increase human capital. In this sense, ties that bind may also come with limitations.

What is clear in the broader network literature is that many aspects of life are affected by the relationships we form in a wide range of networks. Individuals, organizations, and institutions all have networks that facilitate, and sometimes hinder, access to critical resources. Communities with vibrant cross-cutting networks have greater collective efficacy as Sampson (2008) and others have demonstrated. And it is this aspect of social capital that Putnam views as central to the viability of civil society. It is still under debate whether increasing diversity in such communities undermines collective action and reduces social trust. However, in many communities and countries, diversity will continue to grow as migration and thus immigration becomes an ever-present reality. It will demand that we learn to value difference and to extend tolerance. As Putnam (2020: 338) argues, "… we must … stay fiercely committed to the difficult but ever-worthy project of fashioning an American 'we' that is sustainable because it is inclusive." We return to this theme.

5.2 Norms

Norms are also emphasized in Putnam's work on social capital as supporting collective action and a more responsive civil society in which generalized norms of reciprocity prevail. The networks that connect us often support the emergence of reciprocal exchange and more general norms of reciprocity when exchanges are reliable and repeated over time, providing less risk and uncertainty. It is these norms of reciprocity that generate the grounds for collective action in groups and bounded networks. But how they emerge, as we note below, remains somewhat elusive.

Where social norms that do carry force exist, fewer resources are used for monitoring and sanctioning costly endeavors. But they require enforcement if they are to be effective. Enforcement means that at least some third parties are willing to sanction those who do not abide by the existing norms. The emergence and maintenance of sanctioning systems are subject to free-riding problems in that people can benefit from their existence without contributing to their formation or participating in enforcement themselves. As we have noted in Chapter 3, this problem is often referred to as a "second-order" free-riding problem since it focuses on punishing those who do not obey (or contribute). The first-order problem is free-riding on the actual provision of a collective good that benefits the group. Informal rules and norms provide one basis in many settings for moving beyond individual interests to focus on what is good for the collectivity. But less is known about how these norms emerge in the first place and become legitimized, or how prevalent norms change over time to resolve collective action problems.

Over time, however, as history reveals, norms do change. Political scientists and economists have approached this topic often with the use of game theory to analyze the conditions under which changes in acceptable (or unacceptable) behavior lead to alterations in the relevant norms. As Ellickson (2001: 51) argues, "a shift in internal cost-benefit calculations or an alteration of group membership can spur a group to change its informal rules." And a change in informal rules may lead to norm change, particularly if support for the informal rule change is at a "tipping point" (e.g., Cooter 1998), gaining support in the relevant group. A prominent example is the eventual change in norms against smoking that finally reached a tipping point after many years of public health campaigns about the rise in lung cancer deaths attributable to first- or second-hand smoke. In cases like this, and others regarding important social norms, the role of leaders and cascades in behavior have also been explored (e.g., Sunstein 1996) to identify factors that facilitate such norm changes. Reliance on norms, however, has its limitations in instigating and sustaining collective action.

5.3 Trust

One key aspect of social capital is trust, particularly general social trust, which in many sectors of society and in many countries is declining. Polarization along political, ethnic, racial, and even gender lines is not waning, but growing, creating divides not easily crossed. The global coronavirus pandemic alone has exacerbated the extent to which inequality in access to resources (and in this case life-saving vaccines and treatments), so glaringly obvious, is increasing in many corners of the world. Even before the pandemic the erosion of trust not just in others, but in our institutions had begun its downward trajectory. This includes trust in government, business, religious organizations, social media, journalists, and politicians, among others. "Khanna points out that when citizens lack trust, they are less likely to comply with laws and regulations, pay taxes, tolerate different viewpoints or ways of life, contribute to economic vitality, resist appeals of demagogues or support their neighbors" (cited in Lord 2019: 2). Lord continues: "without trust, societies are at risk of chaos and conflict. They are less likely to create and invent."

While this prognosis may overstate the potential role of trust in contributing to solutions to current global crises and the list of maladies identified by Khanna (2018) that limit entrepreneurship in developing economies, general social trust, where it exists, does have positive consequences in social life, not just in terms of economic development. It allows us to engage with and support key institutions, if warranted, that serve society and it creates the grounds for cooperation and ultimately contributes to social order.

What remains unclear in the research we have reviewed is what the source of general social trust is. When do we begin to feel confident enough to trust "strangers," those we do not know and have no history with? If it only comes about primarily due to the existence of background institutions in which we trust (or have confidence in), how do we get to trusted institutions? This conundrum exists in the literature on trust in government, for example. As we have noted in Chapter 4, it is not clear if the ground for general social trust is a trusted government or if we get to trusted government when general social trust is high.

According to Newton (2007: 357) in his analysis of linkages between social trust and political trust, "the good news is ... that social and political institutions and the way they work together have profound implications for social trust, as well as political trust and confidence." He concludes that "trust may well be a top-down phenomenon that is influenced by the nature and operation of social and political institutions, as much as a bottom-up phenomenon built upon patterns of childhood socialization and the life experiences of individual citizens." If his conclusion is correct then our focus going forward should be on shoring up our institutions to make them fair, impartial, and responsive to the citizens they serve.

Factors Newton (2007) finds as evidence of improving generalized social trust include the rule of law, low corruption, effective government, universalistic rather than selective welfare systems, and a working democracy in which people have confidence. As noted in recent press articles, worries about declining support for democratic regimes around the world are rising as autocratic movements gain steam. Confidence in the institutions of government is waning. In the United States, for example, confidence (or trust) in Congress is at an all-time low.[1] Wealthier, more equal societies are notably those that are higher in social trust, providing further evidence of the significance of responsive and just institutions that focus on the well-being of their constituents. The democratic process is central to the success of this project as it assures that the will of the people will determine governmental priorities. But what if citizens lose faith in the process?

5.4   A note on distrust

I have spent little time in this book discussing the role of distrust in the political process and how to cope in places characterized mainly as cultures of distrust. What we know is that once distrust sets in it is much harder to create grounds for trust. What is complicated in the relationship between trust and democracy is that some degree of distrust is baked into our institutions of democracy to make them resilient against abuse of power, even if by those who have been duly elected. The balance of powers across institutions of democracy helps to limit power use. This fact is one reason for trust in government. It is when an imbalance of power exists (as when the executive branch oversteps its legitimate forms of influence) that distrust increases in democratic political systems.

Offe (1999) views a deficit of trust in the institutions of governance, both in democracies of the West and Eastern Europe, post-communism, as problematic. "Without informal modes of coordination, he argues, it is difficult if not impossible to solve the numerous collective-action problems that confront societies today" (Offe cited in Warren 1999b: 6). The scale of these problems requires institutional intervention; they cannot be resolved easily at the level of interpersonal relationships. In a recent survey by the Pew Research Center conducted in 2018, trust in government and each other in the United States has been perceived to be shrinking.[2] One reason this is so important is that in this same survey a majority of Americans see low trust in both the federal government and in each other as making it harder to solve problems.[3] And it is, as we have witnessed in the face of a subsequent pandemic and related global problems. People live in different political spheres and media bubbles, making consensus difficult to achieve and progress on solutions complicated.

5.5   The path forward: tolerance and restoring democratic principles and procedures

The path forward is not at all clear. However, we do know that effective democracies are critical, and tolerance of difference is important. For Misztal (1996: 11), "... to construct conditions in which people learn to deal with one another in a trustworthy way without making everyone feel the same involves the generation of a sense of belonging and participation through the politics of democratization." It is precisely this project that is currently being undermined in many democracies across the globe in the face of increasing immigration to avoid conflicts and migration due to climate change. In the concerns he voiced at the end of the twentieth century with respect to a fragile civil society, Putnam (2000) could not have fully anticipated the coming threats to democracies at home and abroad, fueled by the rise of polarization and the relentless push toward authoritarianism.

In more recent surveys, Dimock (2020: 5), president of the Pew Research Center, notes that the polarization that exists in the United States currently is "about the alignment of nearly all major social and issue divides along the same partisan cleavage, and the much deeper levels of partisan animosity people express about those on the other side." Members of both parties, he reports, now view the opposing side as a "threat to the well-being of the nation." As Putnam (2020: 6) puts it: "Public debates are characterized not by deliberation on differing ideas, but by demonization of those on the opposing side." It is this animosity that undermines trust and confidence in the political system, including the federal government. It is also driving radical groups to "take back" their government, breeding discord and dissension in society, in part a result of a "fractured social media," one rife with misinformation and inaccuracies, not to mention being widely viewed as one-sided by both sides (Dimock 2020).

Misztal (1996: 255) emphasizes the extent to which the very legitimacy of liberal democracies relies heavily on democratic principles and procedures such as free and fair elections and the peaceful rotation of ruling parties. In the United States, these procedures are also under attack with pressures in various parts of the nation to restrict voting rights[4] and put in place politically oriented public servants who might challenge election results if not to their liking, not to mention the rise of militant groups willing to use violence to control the actual outcome of elections (more common in autocracies). Similar threats around the world persist, even for countries that have relatively recently made the transition to more democratic forms of government, such as those in Eastern Europe.

Putnam (2000) originally viewed restoring social capital, primarily through increasing social connections in our associations, neighborhoods, and communities, as important in the fight to renew civil society and shore up our faltering institutions of democracy. For him, we needed to fill those "now empty forums of democracy." In 2020 and beyond the fight is over who controls those forums of democracy – the voices of division and hate or the voices of reason and tolerance. In Misztal's (1996) discussion of trust in modern societies, distrust is viewed as the outcome of intolerance in society and a source of distrust between the state and its citizens. For her, tolerance as a "live and let live" philosophy is no longer sufficient. "Without broadening the notion of tolerance to include mutual understanding and trust, we will be unable to resolve our contemporary problems in such a way as to enhance social cooperation" (Misztal 1996: 228). And she was writing at the end of the twentieth century, prior to the emergence of even greater challenges to democracy that have intensified in recent decades. Uslaner (1999) agrees about the importance of tolerance of those who are different from us, without which society will be more rancorous and less open to compromise. But how we get to a more tolerant society remains a difficult question. Leadership matters, but other factors, historical and cultural, weigh in.

Many factors, some historically and culturally specific, contributed to the "upswing" in the United States during the Progressive Era, the focus of Putnam's book by that name (Putnam 2020). It was initiated not by any single leader or party, but, as he notes, by many everyday citizens using their own influence and efforts to come together to create a change that would lead to a more inclusive, "we-oriented" society. To quote Putnam (2020: 338): "An ideologically diverse generation of Progressive reformers arose who experimented, innovated, organized, and worked for change from the level of the tenement, neighborhood, ward, and union … to the statehouse, the halls of Congress, the Supreme Court, and the White House." It remains to be seen, under the current political and social climate, if a similar broad-based movement is even possible in order to turn the tides of division and cynicism. What would bring us together, short of another attack on U.S. soil as happened post 9/11?

Continuing to diagnose problems with liberal democracies in modern societies, Misztal (1996: 355) writes: "We witness today the political impact of new types of interest organizations and representation, which have been facilitated by the fragmentation of society, the polity, and the economy," leading to a crisis of legitimacy in part due to the rise in what she refers to as alternative forms of authority. This crisis of legitimacy is being witnessed in many countries now being strained by internal conflicts, weakening institutions of government, deep social and political divisions, and global economic pressures, including those derived from a global pandemic. A firm commitment to the rule of law and a reaffirmation of democratic principles in the face of these challenges is required. And we should heed the caution Putnam (2020: 337) issues in his own concluding chapter: "never to compromise on equality and inclusion," or what Warren (1999a) refers to as the ineffable effort to create a new kind of egalitarian pluralism, one that recognizes the real complexities of modern societies.

Affirming or reaffirming democratic principles and processes is unarguably a complex task, riddled with pitfalls. Democratic theorists have focused on this problem for decades and it is particularly relevant when democracies begin to fail. In talking about the relationship between democracy and trust, Warren (1999a) includes a discussion of the strengths and weaknesses of deliberative democracy as one component of resolving basic conflicts that threaten the effectiveness and responsiveness of democracies. He notes that institutions to be trusted must themselves be responsive to communication. "This requires (a) access to information and institutions structured so as to provide the necessary transparency, and (b) institutional means for challenging authorities, institutions and trusted individuals (Warren 1996; Braithwaite 1998)" (Warren 1999a: 338). Only when democracies remain responsive to such challenges do they remain effective and trusted forms of governance. As Warren (1999: 353) concludes, "democracy requires a delicate balance of trust where matters are settled and monitoring of decision-makers where they are not." This balance is hard to achieve.

Social capital has come to mean many things both in theory and in empirical work in the social sciences. As I have argued, the way to make it comprehensible is to look under the umbrella and take it apart, focusing on the networks, norms, and trust included in its definition, treating them as distinct concepts with separate, but sometimes connected, roles in understanding important social and political processes. I hope this book furthers the effort to clarify the significance of this work, recognizing the debt we owe to Robert Putnam, a political scientist, for putting it on our agenda and continuing to be a voice of concern about the maladies facing democracies around the world, but especially here at home.

Notes

1. As Dimock (2020: 6) reports, based on the results of a U.S. Pew Survey, "About three-quarters (74%) say elected officials don't 'care what people like me think' and put their own interests first. And although most see elected officials as intelligent and even patriotic, wide majorities think they are selfish and dishonest."
2. The Pew Research Center Survey of U.S. adults conducted Nov. 27–Dec. 10, 2018, on "Trust and Distrust in America," shows that 75% of Americans believe trust in the federal government has been shrinking and that 64% believe trust in each other is on the decline (https://www.pewresearch.org/politics/2019/07/22/trust-and-distrust-in-america/).
3. In the same "Trust and Distrust in America" Pew Research Center survey in 2018, 64% of Americans think low trust in the government and 70% for trust in each other "makes it harder to solve problems" (https://www.pewresearch.org/politics/2019/07/22/trust-and-distrust-in-america/).
4. In Putnam's (2020: 6) words: "And those in power seek to consolidate influence by disenfranchising voters unsupportive of their views."

References

Braithwaite, John (1998). "Institutionalizing Distrust, Enculturating Trust." Pp. 343–75 in Valerie Braithwaite and Margaret Levi (eds.), *Trust and Governance*. New York: Russell Sage Foundation.

Cohen, Jean (1999). "Trust, Voluntary Association and Workable Democracy: The Contemporary American Discourse of Civil Society." Pp. 108–248 in Mark E. Warren (ed.), *Democracy & Trust*. Cambridge: Cambridge University Press.

Cook, Karen S., Eric R.W. Rice, and Alexandra Gerbasi (2004). "The Emergence of Trust Networks under Uncertainty: The Case of Transitional Economies—Insights from Social Psychological Research." Pp. 193–212 in Susan Rose Ackerman, Bo Rothstein, and Janos Kornai (eds.), *Problems of Post Socialist Transition: Creating Social Trust*. New York: Palgrave Macmillan.

Cooter, Robert D. (1998). "Expressive Law and Economics." *Journal of Legal Studies* 27(2): 585–608.

Dimock, Michael (2020, February 19). "How Americans View Trust, Facts, and Democracy Today." *Trust Magazine*. Washington, DC: Pew Research Center.

Ellickson, Robert C. (2001). "The Evolution of Social Norms: A Perspective from the Legal Academy." Pp. 35–75 in Michael Hechter and Karl-Dieter Opp (eds.), *Social Norms*. New York: Russell Sage Foundation.

Fukuyama, Frances (1995). *Trust: The Social Virtues and the Creation of Prosperity*. New York: Penguin.

Khanna, Tarun (2018). *Trust: Creating the Foundation for Entrepreneurship in Developing Countries*. Oakland, CA: Berrett-Koehler.

Knack, Stephen and Philip Keefer (1997). "Does Social Capital Have an Economic Payoff? A Cross-Country Investigation." *Quarterly Journal of Economics* 112: 1251–88.

Lord, Kristin M. (2019). "Six Ways to Repair Declining Social Trust." *Social Innovation Review* (January 31): 1–8.

Misztal, Barbara (1996). *Trust in Modern Societies*. Cambridge: Polity Press.

Newton, Kenneth (2007). "Social and Political Trust." Pp. 342–61 in Russell J. Dalton and Hans-Dieter Lingemann (eds.), *The Oxford Handbook of Political Behavior*. Oxford: Oxford University Press.

Offe, Claus (1999). "How Can We Trust Our Fellow Citizens?" Pp. 42–87 in Mark E. Warren (ed.), *Democracy & Trust*. Cambridge: Cambridge University Press.

Putnam, Robert D. (2000). *Bowling Alone: The Collapse and Revival of American Community*. New York: Simon & Schuster.

Putnam, Robert D. (2016). *Our Kids: The American Dream in Crisis*. New York: Simon & Schuster.

Putnam, Robert D. (2020). *The Upswing: How America Came Together a Century Ago and How We Can Do It Again*. New York: Simon & Schuster.

Putnam, Robert D. and David E. Campbell (2010). *American Grace: How Religion Divides and Unites Us*. New York: Simon & Schuster.

Putnam, Robert D. and Lewis M. Feldstein (with Don Cohen) (2007). *Better Together: Restoring the American Community*. New York: Simon & Schuster.

Sampson, Robert J. (2008). "Collective Efficacy Theory: Lessons Learned and Directions for Future Inquiry." Pp. 149–67 in Francis T. Cullen, John Paul Wright, and Kristie Blevins (eds.), *Taking Stock: The Status of Criminological Theory* (Advances in Criminological Theory, Vol. 15). New York: Routledge.

Sunstein, Cass (1996). "Social Norms and Social Roles." *Columbia Law Review* 96(4): 903–68.

Uslaner, Eric M. (1999). "Democracy and Social Capital." Pp. 121–50 in Mark E. Warren (ed.), *Democracy & Trust*. Cambridge: Cambridge University Press.

Warren, Mark E. (1996). "Deliberative Democracy and Authority." *American Political Science Review* 90: 45–60.

Warren, Mark E. (1999a). "Democratic Theory and Trust." Pp. 310–45 in Mark E. Warren (ed.), *Democracy & Trust*. Cambridge: Cambridge University Press.

Warren, Mark E. (1999b). "Introduction." Pp. 1–21 in Mark E. Warren (ed.), *Democracy & Trust*. Cambridge: Cambridge University Press.

Index

Titles in the **Elgar Advanced Introductions** series include:

International Political Economy
Benjamin J. Cohen

The Austrian School of Economics
Randall G. Holcombe

Cultural Economics
Ruth Towse

Law and Development
Michael J. Trebilcock and Mariana Mota Prado

International Humanitarian Law
Robert Kolb

International Trade Law
Michael J. Trebilcock

Post Keynesian Economics
J.E. King

International Intellectual Property
Susy Frankel and Daniel J. Gervais

Public Management and Administration
Christopher Pollitt

Organised Crime
Leslie Holmes

Nationalism
Liah Greenfeld

Social Policy
Daniel Béland and Rianne Mahon

Globalisation
Jonathan Michie

Entrepreneurial Finance
Hans Landström

International Conflict and Security Law
Nigel D. White

Comparative Constitutional Law
Mark Tushnet

International Human Rights Law
Dinah L. Shelton

Entrepreneurship
Robert D. Hisrich

International Tax Law
Reuven S. Avi-Yonah

Public Policy
B. Guy Peters

The Law of International Organizations
Jan Klabbers

International Environmental Law
Ellen Hey

International Sales Law
Clayton P. Gillette

Corporate Venturing
Robert D. Hisrich

Public Choice
Randall G. Holcombe

Private Law
Jan M. Smits

Consumer Behavior Analysis
Gordon Foxall

Behavioral Economics
John F. Tomer